Harnessing the
Power of Your Organization for
Breakthrough Success

INNOVATION THE NASA WAY

ROD PYLE

New York Chicago San Francisco Athens London Madrid Mexico City
Milan New Delhi Singapore Sydney Toronto

1 2 3 4 5 6 7 8 9 0 DOC/DOC 1 2 0 9 8 7 6 5 4

ISBN: 978-0-07-182913-7
MHID: 0-07-182913-X

e-ISBN: 978-0-07-182914-4
e-MHID: 0-07-182914-8

Library of Congress Cataloging-in-Publication Data

Pyle, Rod.
Innovation the NASA way : harnessing the power of your organization for breakthrough success / Rod Pyle.
pages cm
ISBN 978-0-07-182913-7 (alk. paper) -- ISBN 0-07-182913-X (alk. paper)
1. United States. National Aeronautics and Space Administration--History 2. Technological innovations--Case studies. 3. Creative thinking--Case studies. I. Title.
TL521.312.N477 2010
658.4'063--dc23

2013049760

To my alma mater, Stanford University.
Thanks for everything that you do.

CONTENTS

FOREWORD

Our nation's investment in NASA returns a wide range of benefits and value to society. These benefits range from the tangible to the abstract. Most often cited examples include direct knowledge of our changing planet, a better understanding of the universe, advancing technology, growing the economy, inspiring future generations, and advancing U.S. global leadership.

The common element that has set NASA apart for generations has been the agency's ability to find innovative ways to deliver each these benefits. Most of us have our favorite stories of innovation at NASA. Most often cited examples include the moon landings, safely bringing home the Apollo 13 crew, saving the Hubble Space Telescope, and many recent successful landings of robots on Mars.

In Innovation the NASA Way, Rod Pyle reminds us of many less-well-known examples of NASA innovation. From the early challenges of hypersonic flight, to spacewalking, to saving the first space station, and to working with the private sector to save our current space station, Pyle identifies specific challenges NASA has faced and then outlines the ultimate solutions worked out by the agency's talented workforce. Each of these examples is a compelling story of innovation as he reminds us that "sometimes innovation is not a technology, not machines, and not anything material. Sometimes it is a thing of the spirit, a core belief and strength."

My belief is that NASA's primary value to society is as an engine of innovation. Reading this book is an affirmation of that belief.

Lori Garver
Former NASA Deputy Administrator

ACKNOWLEDGMENTS

As always, thanks to the many grand people who selflessly donated time and attention to the completion of this book. I could not have done it without your invaluable input. Any errors or oversights remaining are mine.

Specifically and in no particular order, thanks to:

Knox Huston, my spectacular editor at McGraw-Hill Professional, and his long-time friend—and my agent and friend—John Willig of Literary Services Inc.

Ann Pryor, Chelsea Van der Gaag, Scott Kurtz, and many others also at McGraw: thank you so much for your support and talents. You are the best.

Henry Spencer provided amazing services as a fact-checker and proofreader— his contributions were many, and anywhere they were not observed was strictly a matter of available space. His knowledge of the field is apparently limitless. Likewise, factual corrections and observations were contributed by Michael Ciancone, Chris Gamble, Christopher Ramsay, and Stephen Garber, all of current or past NASA affiliation. Steven Dick, formerly of NASA and now the Baruch S. Blumberg NASA/Library of Congress Chair in Astrobiology, was invaluable as always. His remaining professional credits would fill a page, so I'll stop there, but he is a gracious and willing colleague who generously makes time for others.

Roger Launius of the Smithsonian, as always, proffered fine advice. Leonard David, space journalist extraordinaire, lent a hand and an ear. Jason Rhian offered fact- checking and editorial suggestions. Steven Fentress of the Rochester Museum and Science Center provided intelligent observations and is a fine friend. Rand Simberg, fellow space author—thanks for sending me to Henry. Ray Arons of Grumman contributed his knowledge of the Lunar Module.

Janice Alvarez provided tireless and rapid transcription—I would be DOA without her. Jason Clark assisted.

At JPL many people contributed their efforts: Blaine Baggett, Guy Webster (you rule), Rob Manning (ditto), Jia-Rul Cook, Suzanne Dodd, Mark Petrovich, Daniel Goods, Erik Conway, Elena Mejia, Scott Hulme, John Casani, John Beck-Hoffman, and Henry Kline.

Thanks to old friends from my Griffith Observatory days who selflessly donated time to JPL during the *Curiosity* landing: Jim Somers and John Sepikas. And Bob Brooks, who is at JPL every day—your genuine warmth is appreciated.

Peter Orton, who helped both with this and my time at Stanford, is usually the smartest guy in the room. Thanks once again.

Jakob van Zyl, the Associate Director of Product Formulation and Strategy at JPL, granted a lengthy and insightful interview—much appreciated.

Joe Engle corrected the chapter on the X-15 . . . because *he was there*. His wife Jeanie is always a supportive presence.

Richard Godwin, Rick Tumlinson, Bob Richardson, Andrew Nelson, and Alexandra Hall of the NewSpace community, thank you for your kind support and input. You are transforming the face of space exploration. Former Deputy Administrator Lori Garver, your presence at NASA is missed already.

Nick Stevens, über-talented artist, kindly provided his rendering of a NASA-crewed Mars craft design for the cover art—thanks for that.

To my parents and sister—what can I say? Fate and genetics put us together; it was a good call. Gloria Lum, you completed their work—you're a smart and gracious partner. Sherry Clark—thanks for your love and understanding.

Now . . . let's talk innovation. I can't imagine anything else I'd rather do.

CHAPTER 1

CURIOSITY: SEVEN MINUTES OF TERROR

CHALLENGES

- Find a new and innovative way to deliver the heaviest, yet most delicate Mars rover to date to the surface of the Red Planet.
- Build on a history of incremental innovation while taking a huge leap into untested technologies.
- Perform these tasks in a budgetary environment of increasingly scarce resources.
- Live up to the Jet Propulsion Laboratory's (JPL's) reputation for vastly outperforming stated goals and objectives.

The quietude of Mars had been uninterrupted for decades. Except for the occasional furious dust storm, which could rage across Mars and vanish as quickly as it came, the planet was silent as a crypt, red dust whisking along in a forlorn breeze. A tiny sun, only a quarter as bright as that seen from Earth, hung low in the ruddy sky, and sand the color of mud stretched endlessly in all directions. The only other features that were evident were rocks . . . millions of them in all shapes and sizes, but all uniformly the color of rust.

Not far from this place, known on Earth as Chryse Planitia or the Golden Plain, sat a machine, quiet and inert. Covered in a thick layer of brick-colored silt, the metallic carcass of *Viking 1*, one of two U.S. landers from the 1970s, had been idle for 14 years. Its radio dish was rotated toward a footpad covered in sandy drift. An errant command from Earth in 1982 had forced the lander to break contact and stare groundward permanently. For years the machine had continued to function, its small computer waiting for a command from home that never arrived. A small trickle of electric current still flowed from its fading nuclear power supply, but it was now useless, as the onboard computers had long since stopped functioning.

Viking 1, and with it the rest of Mars, felt dead.

Then, barely noticeable overhead, a flickering light slowly circumscribed an arc upward into the cloudless sky, then after a few minutes winked out. Eventually a red-and-white parachute could be seen drifting groundward.

As it came closer, something lowered itself from the huge parachute. Then, in a move straight out of an *X-Files* episode, the tiny thing expanded tenfold in a heartbeat—huge tan bags looking like enormous beach balls inflated instantly as the object continued to fall. A hissing roar announced braking rockets that slowed its final approach, then, with a faint *bang*, the thing was cut loose from its parachute and braking rockets, falling . . . .

And it *bounced*.

It struck Mars and bounced again and again— JPL stopped counting after fifteen. Estimates went as high as thirty. The first bounces sent it almost 50 feet skyward, only to come back to the ground for another rebound. Eventually it rolled to a stop.

It sat for quite a while, and then the air in the brown bags was released with a hissing rush as they deflated. What remained looked like a little pyramid. Then, ever so slowly, one side panel lowered itself toward the ground.

A full Martian day and a frigid night passed as the machine performed silent internal checks. Then, when the ruddy dawn came, a thin whirring noise and a few solenoid clicks heralded the activation of a microwave oven–sized box atop the platform. Restraining straps were cut, and in an agonizingly slow crawl, the first mobile machine on Mars used its six spiked aluminum wheels to crawl down one of the dropped sides of the pyramid. It paused near the bottom of the ramp, then gingerly rolled one wheel onto the red soil.

Pathfinder's rover, *Sojourner*, had touched Mars.

Back on Earth, cheers rang out at the Jet Propulsion Laboratory (JPL) in Pasadena, California. After years of intense and grueling effort, they had done it. It was July 4, 1997, just over two decades since *Viking 1* had landed on Mars on July 20, 1976. For more than 20 years, no American machine had landed on another world. . . until now. Rob Manning, *Pathfinder*'s young chief engineer, was elated, ecstatic, and exhausted. And his day was just beginning.

Manning reflected on how, just a few years earlier, a grumpy chief designer of NASA's Apollo moonship had called the design for *Pathfinder*'s landing system "just plain crazy." It had engendered everything from quiet titters to outright skepticism when it was first presented. Even the normally jocular Manning had squinted and gone silent for a moment when he first saw it. Delicate robotic probes don't bounce to a landing on a distant planet, and they don't then roll to a random stopping point and hope to right themselves. It was crazy, risky, and, to some people, undignified. But Manning and his team soon realized that it was a reliable, energy-efficient, and affordable way to deliver a machine to Mars—a world that disabled or destroyed 65 percent of the machines that dared to venture there.

CHALLENGE:

How to land a probe on Mars that arrives at extreme speeds and must decelerate immediately.

Pathfinder was the product of an informal skunk works at the lab. Designed and built by a deliberately small staff, and on a lean budget, it existed largely under NASA's institutional radar. Given this limited scope, *Pathfinder* had no choice other than to smack directly into Mars, hopefully slowing enough to land intact. *Viking 1* had braked into Martian orbit and allowed controllers to look things over before landing, but *Pathfinder*'s much smaller rocket had to take a direct route to the surface of the Red Planet, immediately making the transition from screaming interplanetary speeds to a flaming entry into the Martian atmosphere, landing like a 600-pound Super Ball.

Pathfinder had been an amazing challenge. The Viking program could not be repeated, probably ever, because of its great expense (about eight billion in today's dollars). This was the "new NASA" under its revolutionary new administrator, Daniel Goldin. "Faster, better, cheaper" was his mantra. Do more with less, and make damned sure it works.

LEAN, MEAN . . . AND SUCCESSFUL

Unfortunately, as almost any engineer from the "faster, better, cheaper" era will tell you, the answer should have been, "Sure; pick any two." Innovation can be encouraged, but not at gunpoint. This policy engendered a series of failures, the repercussions of which were felt for years. But to JPL's everlasting credit, *Pathfinder* was not one of them. It was one of NASA's new "Discovery Program" missions intended to be quick and cheap. The team of young engineers designing the spacecraft was operating in the shadow of a much larger mission, the *Cassini* Saturn probe. That school bus–sized, multibillion-dollar undertaking provided a surprising amount of tactical and political cover, allowing Manning and his team to create a small but ingeniously efficient lander and rover pair that would begin to attract real attention only near the end of its journey to the launchpad. They had been inventing and designing and building and coding so fast that they didn't even have time to properly document most of what they had accomplished. There was no time or money for documentation. Fortunately, the machine worked.

SOLUTION:

Use the simplest and surest methodology to land.
Accept constructive input, and resist habitual negativity.

The little rover was designed to last for 14 days, and its base station for 30. Instead, both objects lasted almost three months, though not without issues. The lander suffered a form of electronic epilepsy: a series of computer panics, when its tiny electronic brain would lock up and reboot spontaneously. It was aggravating as hell, but the engineers kept nursing it back to health. *Sojourner* had its own issues—the little rover tended to drift to the right as it drove around for weeks, sniffing rocks with sensitive devices and exploring a radius of about 30 feet from the lander. But it got where it needed to go—not very far, but for the first of its kind, far enough. Then, on September 27, just under three months after its arrival, the lander died, taking the rover with it.

But the 14-week mission had proven that a mobile probe could be flown to and operated on Mars. In 2004, the twin Mars Exploration Rovers (MERs), each 15 times more massive than *Sojourner*, left Earth headed for the Red Planet. These too bounced to a landing in a fashion identical to *Pathfinder* and conducted an outrageously successful mission—six years for *Spirit* and more than ten (to date) for *Opportunity*. By any measure, the MERs were off the charts. But that was not on Manning's mind now—his team had designed and flown *Pathfinder* and been principal players for MER, but even before the MERs landed on the Red Planet, he had a bigger problem . . . both literally and figuratively. For the next rover, he had to devise a way to land a machine the size of a small car on Mars by 2010 (the date later slipped to 2012), and the bouncy arrival was just not going to work. The team would have to start from scratch to land the one-ton rover, and it made his head hurt.

Rob Manning is a bear of a man, bearded, broad-chested, and ebullient. He is very passionate about his work and about Mars, and he often thinks faster than he can get the words out. He seems much younger than his mid-fifties, the gray frosting of his beard notwithstanding. Anyone who is not his friend soon wants to be. He is an inspirational leader with a keen mind and an engineer's tenacity for problem solving. And he now had the problem of a career to solve: How do you land something the size and weight of a small Toyota on Mars? As the chief engineer of *Curiosity* and a key member of the entry, descent, and landing (EDL) team, he knew that the success or failure of *Curiosity*'s arrival on Mars would rest on a handful of shoulders. He felt the pressure keenly.

A NEW APPROACH

The Mars Science Laboratory, known more popularly as *Curiosity* (after the rover's name), was launched on November 26, 2011, but the mission design had been underway since before 2000. The machine was huge and vastly more complex than previous rovers. It would use a nuclear power source instead of solar panels to support an amazing array of cutting-edge sensing and analysis equipment. Its robotic arm was also far more sophisticated than those of its forebears, with vastly improved versions of the scientific instruments that had gone before, some new cameras, and, perhaps most remarkably, a drill and soil scoop. This was going to be one for the record books.

But all this came with a staggering weight penalty, and not since Viking had something so heavy and massive been sent off to Mars. At more than 2,000 pounds (the MER rovers had weighed 385 pounds), it was simply huge. Add to that the increased complexity and delicacy of the machine, and a beach-ball landing simply would not work. Additionally, the scientists wanted a pinpoint landing. Getting this beast to a target on Mars in one piece was a world-class problem.

CHALLENGE:

To land on Mars with nearly 10 times the accuracy of any previous mission.

An additional issue was accuracy. The landing zones for Mars-bound landers were always mapped as an ellipse-shaped area of acceptable destinations. *Pathfinder*'s landing ellipse had been a generous 124 miles long—if the machine bounced and rolled to a stop somewhere in that 124- by 50-mile area, the landing would be considered "on target." For the Mars Exploration Rovers, the ellipse had shrunk to 93 miles by 12—still a large area and bigger than many U.S. counties. For *Curiosity*, which would be landing within a crater with high walls and a mountain in the center, the ellipse was a miserly 12 miles by 4 . . . small, considering that the lander had to arrive there after crossing some 150 million miles of space and entering the atmosphere at 13,000 miles per hour. It was like threading a needle with rope.

When Manning and his team began to consider new ways to deliver *Curiosity* to Mars in one piece, they rapidly discovered that the brain trust that had designed the Viking landers was largely gone. So were the very expensive rocket engines that had slowed those machines to a soft landing. Armed with little more than a handful of incomplete plans, they contacted Aerojet, the company that had built Viking's landing rockets, and gave it the task of building a new throttlable rocket engine that was powerful enough to land *Curiosity* in one piece.

But there was far more to the problem than that. The mission had a set of landing constraints that Viking's designers had barely touched upon. For one thing, nobody wanted rocket exhaust to contaminate the landing area or blow red dust and gravel up onto the rover's sensitive instrumentation. There were also engineering considerations—Viking's engines had been mounted on the sides of the lander, and once it arrived, the spent rockets merely sat there, empty and useless, as the unmoving probe worked from one spot. But *Curiosity* was a rover and had to be able to drive for a dozen or more miles around the landing zone, ultimately arriving at the base of a peak in the crater's center, about seven miles distant. Dragging a bunch of heavy, unneeded descent engines along was a nonstarter.

And then there were what the engineers call "flight dynamics"—that is, keeping the thing upright in the air—to worry about. Viking had had three large landing legs to set down on Mars, and much of its weight had been at the bottom of the spacecraft, below the level of the engines. The other rovers had arrived on a landing stage with a weight distribution similar to Viking's. *Curiosity*'s center of gravity was much higher, with a heavy nuclear fuel source high atop the rear of the rover and the equally heavy instrumented robotic arm and camera mast extending from the front of the machine. The center of gravity, the point around which the lander could pivot disastrously during landing, was high—dangerously high. Descending with engines mounted on the obvious spot—the sides or bottom of the rover—would be like balancing a bowling ball on a broomstick. If it toppled to one side, scratch one $2.5 billion rover.

One final issue burned in everyone's minds: unlike with Viking and MER, each of which had landed twin spacecraft on Mars, there was only enough money for one *Curiosity.* There would be no second chance—if the single rover failed to land safely, that would be that. It would crash, the mission would be over, and, given the state of the U.S. space program in the twenty-first century, the entire Mars exploration effort would probably die with it.

It felt as if all the conditions surrounding the mission were conspiring against its success. Manning sometimes felt like the British soldiers he had seen in the movies of his youth, back-to-back in a circle and surrounded by hostiles. It was not an enviable position, and only truly innovative, out-of-the-box thinking would allow *Curiosity*'s escape.

NO SECOND CHANCES

The sequence they needed to design was encapsulated in one benign-sounding acronym: EDL, for entry, descent, and landing. But the blandness of the term belied its complexity: there were no second chances, no do-overs. *Seven minutes of terror.*

SOLUTION:

Use lessons learned from older missions combined with daring new ideas to design a system that would lower the machine, delicately and on target. Accept a calculated risk to innovate for accuracy.

Many ideas were considered, and most of them were soon rejected. They either did not meet mission requirements, were way too expensive, or were just too risky. Other designs lived longer lives in the marathon technical meetings but were ultimately deemed unworkable or insufficiently reliable. Then one notion—crazy, scary, and improbable—took root. It would come to be known as sky crane.

Actually, sky crane looked fairly sane until you got to the last act. *Curiosity* would enter the Martian atmosphere screaming along at 19,000 feet per second, and thin as the Martian atmosphere, slamming into even tenuous air at that speed was a big deal. So the spacecraft would have a heat shield even larger than that used in the Apollo program of the 1960s. This shield was shaped in such a way as to allow *Curiosity* to "surf" along the upper atmosphere, gliding to reduce speed.

Then, after its fiery trip through the atmosphere, *Curiosity* would deploy a 50-foot-wide parachute designed to withstand the stresses of supersonic forces—the spacecraft would still be traveling at 900 miles per hour when it unfurled. That would require a lot of testing, but it could probably be achieved.

About 15 seconds later, the heat shield would pop free, and *Curiosity* would be ready for the really hard part: touchdown. Well over nine-tenths of the speed had been scrubbed off by now, but those last few miles were critical to success. This is where it got *really* tricky.

Straddling the rover itself would be a rocket pack—it looked like a huge backpack with eight of those new Aerojet rocket engines sticking out the sides. They would fire, reducing *Curiosity*'s mad velocity to a survivable rate. The rockets would slow the rover to nearly a hover almost exactly 66 feet above Mars. But the wildest bit was yet to come. Once at a relative standstill, *Curiosity* would fire small pyrotechnic devices—retainers made from explosives—to separate from the rocket pack. Finally, and this is where the real weirdness began, the rover would be *lowered* from the hovering rocket pack by four tethers. The rover's suspension system would then drop and lock the wheels in place; they would serve double duty as landing gear. When the wheels sensed surface contact, the rover would pop the lines loose, and the rocket pack would fly away like a startled crow to crash some miles distant, its job done.

CHALLENGE:

Convince upper management—and your peers—that a complex, difficult-to-explain system would work.

Huh? Each engineer, flight specialist, scientist, and, most important, NASA bureaucrat who saw this had his or her own individual reaction. Many blanched; some chuckled; others sucked wind and held it. This was a wild design, with a few hundred things that could go wrong (the landing sequence alone used 79 pyrotechnic devices—the little explosives—just to get to the surface). All it would take was for one of those things to fail and bye-bye, *Curiosity.*

Let's see: one of the little maneuvering rockets could clog, fail to ignite, or explode (it happens) . . . or an explosive bolt could fail to fire (any of the above) . . . or the parachute could tangle or even tear (it had done just that during the endless testing, sometimes ripping almost in two). That would mean a bad afternoon on Mars.

Manning's team convinced management that those risks were acceptable. But there were more. The rockets could fail to throttle properly, and varying their thrust was critical to success. Or the wheels might get hung up and not unfold and lock properly. The tethers that were to lower the rover might get snarled or unspool unevenly. The rocket pack might continue to descend, ever so slightly, during the sky crane maneuver, smashing into the top of *Curiosity.* The computer or sensing devices could get confused and send an erroneous command, allowing the heavy rover to crash.

But somehow, the worst scenario seemed to be in that very last stage of the operation. If just one of the tethers between the rover and the rocket pack failed to separate, *Curiosity* could be yanked over onto its side and ingloriously dragged a few hundred yards before the rockets ran out of fuel and crashed miles away, still leashed to the now-crippled rover. This seemed the most undignified and tragic of all scenarios. At least if the parachute failed, the spacecraft would impact, creating a nice crater and total destruction. But to be dragged by a single string . . .

Ruminating over possible disaster is useful only if it helps to reduce risk. After a certain point, once everything had been tested and tested again, one had to say, "Enough is enough," and trust the design. Or, as Manning put it shortly before the 2012 landing when asked if he was worried about it, "I can't think of anything that *should* go wrong."

SOLUTION:

Think boldly, be daring, exhibit confidence, and, above all, test *everything*. Ducking the potential for failure can lead to disaster.

There were many moments of truth during testing. This was key, just as it had been for *Pathfinder* and the MER rovers. Test, test, test. When it broke, test it again; if it didn't break, figure out why, and then validate that with . . . another test. They tested the parachute, which ripped itself to shreds for quite some time until they got it right. They tested the rocket pack, but even success was only moderately convincing, since they were operating on Earth, a very different environment from Mars. They tested the deployment system for the rover, the heat shield, and the wheels and suspension it would land on. But the one thing they could *not* test was the sky crane itself—Mars has about one-third of Earth's gravity and just a fraction of its atmospheric density. There was just no way to properly simulate sky crane's lowering-via-tethers operation on Earth. They did lower the thing from a helicopter a few times, but it was not the same as what it would go through on Mars. It would simply have to do.

SUCCESS ON MARS

On August 5, 2012, it was game time. After months of cruising the dark void of interplanetary space, *Curiosity* hurtled into the Martian atmosphere. The "seven minutes of terror" had begun. On the ground, tense controllers could only watch passively as the events scrolled down their screens. Because of the distance between Mars and Earth, some 70 million miles away, the radio messages from *Curiosity* were delayed by about 15 minutes. Whatever the controllers saw and heard had already happened "up there." The probe was either already down safely or shrapnel scattered across a few miles of Mars.

Despite this, at JPL, the landing had a very real-time feel to it. You just couldn't help but get caught up in it, and Manning was. But his work, and that of his able team, was done for the moment; the design would either succeed or fail. So he spent a few hours before landing on JPL's TV channel (part of NASA TV) being interviewed about the mission ("It's just a fantastic spacecraft . . . really great, and I had a wonderful team . . . *I can't think of anything that* should *go wrong.*").

He waited out the landing with everyone else.

Telemetry indicated that *Curiosity* was plummeting into the Martian atmosphere. It began to glide in the proper direction, aided by radar and small maneuvering thrusters. The parachute deployed and held, and the heat shield dropped away as planned. Finally, the rocket motors began to fire, slowing the lander's velocity to the critical 1.7 miles per hour. As *Curiosity* neared the surface of Mars, the rockets throttled to the proper thrust to slow almost to a hover.

A deathly silence enfolded the room as controllers gripped their desktops, chair arms, or whatever was handy, knuckles white and bloodless. And then, in tones almost comically calm, the announcement came: "Sky crane deploying." The rocket pack was hovering, the tethers unspooling.

And then—touchdown.

Curiosity had made it—it was on the sands of Mars. The rocket pack separated and flew away to crash-land a few hundred yards distant, and the rover sat, alone and quiet, smack-dab in the middle of the landing ellipse . . . right where they wanted it. Checkouts began and preparation to raise the camera mast commenced, but the terror was over. The damn thing had worked.

About an hour later, during a press conference in the JPL auditorium, a din could be heard from outside. The public relations officer looked up from her notes, bemused and curious. Heads turned en masse, as hardened journalists wondered if they were missing a story outside the room. And then it could be heard: the 100-plus members of the entry, descent, and landing team, all exhausted but elated, had left the control center and were dancing across the wide JPL quad, chanting and fist-pumping in wild exaltation at the top of their lungs: *"E-D-L! E-D-L!! E-D-L!!"*

Boldness. Daring. Passion. The team of designers, scientists, and engineers at JPL and the other NASA centers who designed this mission wore these qualities like a medal, standing tall with pride. After all, the worst thing that could have happened would have been failure . . . and the only thing worse than *that* would have been to not try.

INNOVATIONS

- First, small steps: learn to fly landers and rovers to Mars without entering Martian orbit; use the shortcut of direct trajectory from Earth to the surface of Mars.
- Deliver a small prototype rover to Mars via a new and untried system: bouncing to a stop on a dozen airbags. Operate fast and lean, and stay below top management's radar when and reasonable.

- Follow this with two larger rovers using similar but vastly enhanced technologies.
- Finally, use the lessons learned with these programs to design the largest, most sophisticated rover ever flown.
- Because of this increased mass, draw from 30-year-old experiences with Viking landers to design a new and innovative landing system to deliver this machine to Mars with technologies that could not be tested on Earth.

CHAPTER 2

RED MOON

CHALLENGES

- Build, within a tight time frame, a rocket and satellite to match the Soviet achievement with *Sputnik*.
- Based on this success, leapfrog past planned incremental rocket designs and build the largest, most powerful, and most complex machine in history, the Saturn V booster.
- Manage a national team of contractors, each with its own corporate culture, welding them into a broadly cohesive team to reach the goal of landing a man on the moon before the end of the 1960s.

A SHOCK FROM THE EAST

The first gusts of the coming winter chilled the air in Huntsville, Alabama, on October 4, 1957. Of course, to a man who had come here from the forests of eastern Germany via the deserts of New Mexico, this was a welcome change. Wernher von Braun and his relocated German rocket colleagues thought it a distinct improvement—it felt much more like home.

That afternoon, von Braun had just returned to his office to wrap up the day before heading off to an evening of cocktails and dinner with colleagues. Moments before, he had finished giving the newly nominated secretary of defense a tour of the Redstone Arsenal, the new home of his German rocket team. As he was preparing to leave, the phone rang—it was a reporter from New York.

"What do you think of it?"

"Think of what?" von Braun responded with genuine curiosity.

"The Russian satellite, the one they just orbited."

Von Braun went silent.

The first man-made object was now in space . . . and it was a Soviet creation.

It was distressing, but it was not a surprise. Von Braun and his cadre had known it was coming, but all they had been able to do was wait and watch. The U.S. government was not keen on having former Nazis put up the first American satellite, no matter how qualified they might be. Memories of burning cities and grieving survivors in London and Antwerp, victims of von Braun's V2 missiles, were still far too vivid.

The news of the Soviet triumph had flashed across the globe, but nowhere was it felt more keenly than in this small southern U.S. town. America's archrival had orbited a small satellite, *Sputnik 1*, just this day. It was a two-foot-wide metal sphere with four antennae trailing behind it, and it had little more than a radio transmitter to distinguish it. Still, as the first man-made item to orbit the Earth, it might as well have been an ocean liner in space. The impact was that great.

To the Germans in Huntsville, it was particularly galling. Every 90 minutes, the irritating ball wheeled overhead, sending out a regular beep via its small radio, which was being monitored by governments and amateur radio operators worldwide. It was like a little ambassador for communism saying, "Here I am; the USSR reigns supreme!" The rocket men from Germany did not like it one bit, and none of them were more frustrated than von Braun, who had been lobbying the U.S. government for funds to surpass Soviet efforts for years.

Since coming to the United States after World War II, von Braun had been shuffled about. The government knew that it would need him and his team; it just was not sure where to store them until that time. Moving between Texas and New Mexico, they spent their time flying V2 rockets assembled from parts captured at the close of the war. That program slowed when one of the missiles had the bad taste to crash-land in a cemetery just across the border in Mexico, killing nobody, but making a mess of the graveyard. Washington soon moved the team to Huntsville, to the army's Redstone Arsenal, home of the growing U.S. nuclear missile deterrent. Here the Germans had made a new home and prepared to ascend to the stars as they had hoped to do back in Germany before the madness of the Third Reich.

Whatever else people might say about von Braun, he was a visionary. Born into an aristocratic family at the dawn of World War I, he was an uninspired student until he was bitten by the rocket bug as a teen. Then he knuckled down to his studies and excelled. Tall, handsome, and of baronial bearing, he could charm the stars off the surliest Army general. This turned out to be a useful trait, because once he had completed his engineering studies, young Wernher had built rockets for Hitler that led to the V2, a terror weapon that killed thousands across Europe. Worse, he had joined the Nazi party and been given SS rank by Himmler early in the war (he claimed that he had been forced to accept the honor, but this was never verified). But America's generals needed him to help them catch up with the Soviet Union's missile program, and he needed the blessing of those generals to achieve his dream of flying into space with his rockets.

Von Braun and his team had been busy remaking captured V2s into improved versions that were ultimately known as the

Redstone, America's first deployable nuclear missile. But von Braun wanted no more involvement with weapons—he was aiming for the stars, and the first step was to put a satellite into Earth orbit. He was ready; he had the designs and the basic technology at hand. He had been refining his ideas and the engineering on his own time, and he had been unofficially conducting flight experiments as "nose cone reentry tests" (he had been forbidden to tinker with satellites). But qualified though he might have been, some within the U.S. government had a problem with having a former Nazi building America's first satellite, reformed or not. So the project had gone to the U.S. Navy and its Vanguard rocket.

CHALLENGE:

How to move ahead with an innovative program when powers beyond your control are holding you back.

And then *Sputnik* happened. Panic gripped the American people and much of the free world. The United States had been the supreme victor on two battlefronts in World War II, had fought the Chinese to a standstill in Korea, and had, after all, developed the first atomic weapons. But in an instant, *Sputnik* changed the public relations balance: America was in decline, and the Union of Soviet Socialist Republics was ascendant. It was downright embarrassing, and to many people it constituted a national emergency.

SOLUTION:

Sometimes you must wait for outside intervention, but be prepared to move ahead with your innovation quickly.

RESPONDING . . . WITH FAILURE

So the Navy accelerated the *Vanguard* program. The team responsible had been fiddling with it since 1955, and now the need to flex the West's space muscles was profound. Never mind that the present *Vanguard* satellite was the size of a grapefruit and had little more science onboard than *Sputnik* (it did have temperature sensors, which was *something*); never mind that it was only about 3 pounds to the first Sputnik's 186 pounds. There was a great deal at stake here. Russia had innovated big-time, and America appeared to be standing still.

> **CHALLENGE:**
>
> Respond to the Soviet accomplishment—and quickly.

In a rushed affair before a swath of invited media, the Navy attempted to launch its baby satellite on December 6. There was an expectant hush, then the voice of the launch controller counting backward—a small flash at the tail of the rocket, then the smoke and fury of America's righteous comeback as the rocket left the launchpad. It lifted four feet before the booster crumpled under its own weight and exploded in a mighty fireball that was instantly flashed via TV to living rooms all over America. The pathetic satellite, dinged and dented but still transmitting, was blown clear and reportedly rolled to an inglorious stop under a nearby dumpster.

Sputnik beeped from space; *Vanguard* beeped from underneath a Florida trash can.

The next day, world headlines carried titles such as "Kaputnik!," "Flopnik," and worse. In desperation, President Eisenhower, who not so long ago had defeated the very war machine that created von Braun's V2 rockets, relented and turned to the U.S. Army and its German rocketeers. *"How fast can you get some goddamn thing into orbit?"* they were asked. With admirable restraint, von Braun repeated what he had been saying for almost two years: just give the word, and I'll have one up in 60 days.

While he prepared, the Soviets launched *Sputnik 2*, which weighed more than a *half ton* and carried a dog named Laika into orbit, where it stayed for five months. Laika was not so fortunate, dying from overheating within hours, but that was not the point: Russia had done it again, and on a grand scale. It was not lost on Western militaries that rockets with payloads the size of *Sputnik 2* could potentially carry a small nuclear warhead.

Undeterred, von Braun continued to work on his booster. Meanwhile, in California, the Jet Propulsion Laboratory hurriedly built a new satellite called *Explorer 1*. It looked like a white skyrocket, was only about four feet long, and weighed 30 pounds. But it did carry some scientific instruments and, more important, would be ready when von Braun's rocket was. On January 31, 1958, a beautiful sight was seen above Cape Canaveral in Florida: America's first satellite headed into orbit. It would stay there until 1970, measuring radiation fields around the Earth (*Explorer 1* discovered the Van Allen belts, which help to protect Earth from space-borne radiation).

SOLUTION:

Push past U.S. bureaucratic and political obstacles to use the right people for the right job: von Braun's German rocket team.

This was America's comeback, small though it was. Both countries flew more satellites before 1960, but then came the next Big Embarrassment: the launch of a Soviet citizen, Yuri Gagarin, into orbit in 1961.

This was soon matched by the U.S. flights of Project Mercury—first with Alan Shepard's and Gus Grissom's 15-minute suborbital flights, then with John Glenn's orbital mission. NASA was moving ahead quickly. Von Braun was more than ready for the challenge, living as he was on the cutting edge of rocketry since the 1930s, transforming amateur rocketry into real development programs. While laboring within the Nazi regime, he had been developing techniques and ideas that ultimately translated into NASA's manned space program.

INNOVATION FROM THE OLD WORLD

In terms of management, von Braun brought with him ideas that did not always fit neatly into U.S. military culture. These included ideas that he called "teamwork," "dirty-hands engineering," and "automatic responsibility." The first is obvious: work together to get results (always a good thing when the Gestapo was watching). The second, "dirty hands," meant simply that: engineers, no matter how highly placed, needed to understand everything about their area of responsibility and be willing to roll up their sleeves and get involved right on the shop floor, if necessary. The third, "automatic responsibility," was perhaps the hardest to understand and implement.

CHALLENGE:

How to get the most out of "New World" workers using "Old World" values.

As von Braun described it, each person must "have full cognizance and responsibility for all efforts that fall within the purview of their respective disciplines. . . . [The lab director] is expected automatically to participate in all projects that involve his discipline and to carry his work through to its conclusion." More succinctly, this meant that there was no "my job" versus "your job"—it was simply "our job," and you were expected to make sure that it was a success. This was an intentional blurring of administrative lines, and it had the effect of allowing people to weigh in on an issue that was outside their area of expertise and in a department other than their own. This brought a fresh, outside view to a problem. If a mechanical engineer saw issues involving something that was normally within the purview of the electrical engineers, he was expected to report it and, if necessary, apply himself to developing a solution before moving on. This was not business as usual within the military bureaucracy that surrounded von Braun's operation at the time, but it worked, it stuck, and it became the management backbone of Marshall Space Flight Center (MSFC), NASA's new name for the Redstone Arsenal.

SOLUTION:

Combine "Old World" thinking with new management techniques: everyone is responsible for everything.

Von Braun further minimized the separation of management at the MSFC. Each lab director or senior manager prepared a weekly report. Von Braun read them all, made comments, and was aware of almost everything that was happening under him. He then returned copies of *all* the annotated reports to *all* the managers, so that each one would see what everyone else was doing, and what von Braun thought of it. This kept all his senior people in the loop, aware of what was happening across the board. It also let them all know what his expectations were, for not only did they see one another's reports, but they all saw von Braun's responses to their peers. Finally, it encouraged lateral communication between departments that were in a position to help one another, instead of letting them duck or avoid problems outside their fiefdom. The final result was exemplary and was a critical component in America's effort to reach the moon. Either you solved your problem or you communicated it clearly and quickly to your superior to involve him in reaching a resolution. Nothing languished, and nothing was overlooked or hidden, at least in theory. Communication was immediate, and it was both vertical and horizontal. There were to be no secrets in von Braun's directorate. If there was a downside, it was the occasional slowing of action while a subordinate waited for information to move upward and then waited until it made the return trip back down. But overall, theory and practice were remarkably close in the end.

Central to the implementation of this structure was von Braun's own personality. His interactions were remarkably consistent, whether he was speaking to a subordinate or to the NASA administrator. He was charismatic and friendly to his superiors, and compassionate and encouraging to his subordinates. This won him great loyalty and respect throughout. And while he could "pound the table" when needed, he saved this for extreme occasions, and by doing so amplified the power of that action. In short, true to his aristocratic upbringing in interwar Prussia, he was a gentleman in the classic mold.

CHALLENGE:

How to manage leaders, workers, and processes in off-site locations so that they meet exacting standards.

There was another management technique that von Braun would enhance once the Apollo program got rolling, and he called it "earthquake prediction." Simply put, about 10 percent of the Marshall staff would eventually be sent out to the contractors (who were building the flight hardware) as observers and inspectors (von Braun called them his "sensors"). When they saw a problem, they communicated it to the Marshall center immediately. Of course, the contractors initially were not pleased with this system (which they perceived as spies from the client), and there was early resistance to it, but in these unique circumstances the system worked well, and most contractors ultimately valued the partnership. It's worth noting that there is a fine line between partnership and interference. Not everyone can pull it off, but von Braun managed to.

SOLUTION:

Carefully merge your own employees into relevant contractor operations.

THE DIRTY RAG

By the time America landed men on the moon, there were contractors in all 50 states, and von Braun had operatives stationed at the largest of them. He also made sure that anything that was critical to the safe operation of the Saturn V—*his* Saturn V—went through the engineers at Marshall. The rocket's first stage was built by Boeing at Marshall, then later at NASA's Michoud plant in Louisiana, and the Marshall technicians were in both plants in force. The S-II (second) stage came from North American Aviation in Los Angeles, and when it got to the East Coast, the Marshall engineers were there, disassembling and checking everything like hungry ants. The S-IVB (third) stage was built by McDonnell-Douglas, also in Los Angeles, and it also went through German hands before being incorporated into the rocket.

The most difficult pairing was between Marshall's engineers and North American Aviation. Once the company had completed an S-II stage, von Braun had the assemblies sent directly to Huntsville. There the German engineers would completely disassemble, inspect, and reassemble the five rocket engines one by one. This rankled North American's management—they felt that it was insulting and unnecessary, and that the delays it caused were criminal. They were checking and testing these engines before they left the West Coast, so why do so again at Huntsville? The executives demanded a meeting with von Braun and NASA to correct what they felt was a costly bit of technical meddling.

CHALLENGE:

Convince industry partners to cooperate in the enhancement of quality control across two different working cultures.

From here the story gains almost mythical stature, as it has been repeated so many times by engineers and managers who would savor such an opportunity. It's known as the "greasy rag story." When the North American executives finally met with the NASA team, one of von Braun's key men, Eberhard Rees, greeted them from the head of the conference table with an icy Germanic stare. The man was known as being colder than liquefied oxygen. The North American executives sat, unruffled, their narrow ties knotted at the throats of their starched white shirts. One man spoke up to ask why the hell the Marshall engineers needed to slow down the momentum of the program by tearing apart each and every Saturn S-II stage. Rees heard him out, then pulled a greasy rag from his pocket and dropped it onto the table. All eyes swiveled to the rag, lying there in a soiled heap. Rees surveyed the room, glancing at the rag, which he clearly regarded as he might a lump of excrement. "This is the kind of stuff we find in these engines," he said, turning his reptilian gaze to the assembled executives. It had been left inside a combustion chamber—sloppy work to say the least in a business where microns made the difference between success and disaster. There was a stunned, embarrassed silence (what was there to say?), and the meeting moved on to other matters before adjourning awkwardly. North American reportedly never complained about engine disassembly and inspection again.

SOLUTION:

Use a powerful visual illustration, metaphorical or literal, to make your point.

UNPARALLELED SUCCESS

By 1965, major parts of the Saturn V were undergoing rigorous testing, and in 1967, unmanned flight tests began with *Apollo 4*. At this time, NASA did exercise a rare intervention to override von Braun's cautious nature. The Marshall team had wanted incremental tests of the Saturn, flying the first stage with water ballast in the second and third stages, then launching both the first and second stages fueled, with water ballast in the third, and so forth. But time was running out; intelligence reports hinted that the Soviets were making great strides in their own lunar program. Apollo management in Houston insisted that the Saturn V be tested "all-up," or all at once—just fly all the stages hot and see what happens. Von Braun relented, and after two successful tests, the massive booster was declared ready for prime time. In 1968 the Saturn V, flying for only the third time, lofted its first crew on the *Apollo 8* mission, reaching the moon on Christmas Eve. In the 10 crewed flights of the Saturn V, while there were a few minor malfunctions, the rocket always delivered its crews to Earth orbit and sped them to the moon with a perfect safety record (the *Apollo 13* crisis was a result of an explosion in the capsule's life-support system). In pure percentages, its accomplishments are unparalleled to this day. Von Braun's program stands as a monument to excellence in leadership, enlightened management, and innovation.

INNOVATIONS

- Secretly developing the capability to launch a satellite—despite being ordered not to.
- Building on the success of that program to create the largest rocket in history, the Saturn V.
- Welding a team of contractors into a cohesive whole to build this complex and futuristic machine.
- Implementing a management system, one of the largest and most complex in history, to oversee not only the operations at Huntsville but ultimately the offsite prime contractors as well.
- Finding the balance between incremental testing and faith in the technology that would allow the first manned moon landing to take place before the end of the decade.

CHAPTER 3

RIDING THE FIRE: THE X-15

CHALLENGES

- Design and build an aircraft to explore the hypersonic realm of upper-atmosphere flight, up to Mach 6, using 1950s technology operating right at the edge of its capability.
- Build a cooperative management structure incorporating NASA (and its predecessor), the Air Force, and the U.S. Navy.
- Train pilots to fly in this realm, using stick-and-rudder techniques in the atmosphere and experimental maneuvering rocket technology in space.
- Design and build an aircraft capable of reentering Earth's atmosphere and gliding back, unpowered, to a runway.

FIFTY-ONE FEET OF MEAN

Standing near it was almost like being in the presence of a living thing. In the predawn darkness, he could make out a long, low, and undeniably evil-looking shape shrouded in mist and fog. Then came an errant desert breeze, the ground-hugging clouds of super-chilled oxygen parted, and the world's first spacecraft faded into view bracketed by a desert sunrise.

He stopped and took in the scene. The X-15 looked like 51 feet of barely restrained fury. It was all business, and it looked more like a weapon than a research airplane. The narrow 22-foot wingspan only accentuated the comparison. It was one mean-looking machine, and it was every bit as fast—and as dangerous—as it appeared.

The rocket plane sat in the predawn shadow of its B-52 carrier plane. The former nuclear bomber's right wing had been modified to carry the X-15 dangling from a release mechanism. To the layman, it may have looked ad hoc, but it worked—not without some drama at times, but it worked.

Joe Henry Engle, the 32-year-old test pilot who would be taking the X-15 up for this altitude run, savored the sight. For some reason, looking at this beast, the pinnacle of aircraft development in 1964, he thought back to the small toy airplane his sister had made him out of tin cans when he was eight years old. His mother would not let him play with it because of all the sharp edges . . . and now he was playing with this rocket, which was nothing *but* sharp edges, literally and figuratively. Life had a funny way of circling back sometimes. God, he loved flying.

He climbed the wheeled ladder and settled into the cockpit. It was a tight fit, but he felt comfortable there. Once he was strapped in and connected to the onboard oxygen supply, the canopy was lowered into place and latched shut. Soon the cockpit would be flooded with pure nitrogen, and he would be unable to open his helmet or he would suffocate within moments. He took the opportunity to enjoy a leisurely scratch of his nose before he had to button up his visor.

Looking outside, he reflected on how *different* this aircraft was. The canopy had two *small* windows—slits really—that allowed some sideways and forward visibility, but that was about it. No part of the plane's exterior was visible from inside, and when you were landing, you had to bank to see anything below you. It was not the place for a claustrophobe.

Before him was a display that was not dissimilar to those on the fighter planes it had been his job to test until he entered this program. Some of the more than 130 gauges could be inside a fighter, reporting pressures, rates, temperatures, and a dozen other measurements that were critical to a pilot's survival. Others indicated things that were specific to a rocket that flew beyond the atmosphere and into the fringes of outer space. It was complicated and beautiful.

He completed his 120-step checklist while others worked down their own versions. Then, after one last preflight check from the ground, the turbojets just above him spun up to a dull roar and the bomber headed down the runway, with his spacecraft hanging under the wing. It was almost showtime.

ODD BEDFELLOWS

In the early 1950s, the U.S. government wanted to build a plane that could fly at hypersonic speeds and reach space. Much had been learned since the time of the first supersonic rocket plane, the X-1. That had ultimately been a successful craft, and Chuck Yeager's experience battling the controls as his X-1 was buffeted violently at near Mach 1 speeds had been instructive. Subsequent X-planes had tested other design technologies, and the recipient of this education was to be the X-15.

> **CHALLENGE:**
>
> How to manage a high-performance, exotic program combining the strengths of available government organizations.

Also new was the management structure overseeing the X-15 program. Prior efforts had been pretty basic: NASA's predecessor, the National Advisory Committee for Aeronautics (NACA), a government research outfit with headquarters in Langley, Virginia, had sidled up to the Army Air Force (AAF) to break the sound barrier shortly after World War II. In 1947, the AAF became the U.S. Air Force, but the NACA stayed on until 1958. This fruitful partnership would be ramped up for the X-15.

This arrangement, while it had its challenging moments, would become a sterling model of collaboration—in this case, between NASA, the Air Force, the U.S. Navy, and the aerospace industry. With a few exceptions, and only a couple of major ones, these odd bedfellows cooperated and even supported one another in this high-performance program from 1955 to 1968. Notably absent was congressional oversight and legislative-branch meddling—there was a small but generally quiet oversight board, and that was the extent of it. This was a well-designed civilian-military-industry partnership that, in general, let each organization contribute from its strengths. NASA contracted and flew the rocket planes, the Air Force contributed funds and handled facilities and most logistics, and the Navy also gave money as well as overseeing simulation and training. These assignments evolved over time, but the work was completed with competence (and a minimal amount of interagency struggle).

The only other time a collaboration of this scale was attempted in human spaceflight was the space shuttle. NASA was instructed to coordinate with the Air Force early on to determine shuttle orbiter design specs that would allow for military uses. Despite the fact that this was a smaller overlap than the X-15 project had been, the results nearly killed the shuttle program. But that's a story for another chapter.

As you may suspect, the X-15 collaboration had effects beyond funding and the division of responsibility. In 1958, the NACA was transformed into NASA (which brought new characteristics into being, including moving from what had been basically a research role into a contracting and "flying" entity), and thus the Air Force was now working with a new, small, energetic, and largely untried partner. With its experience in the X-1 and follow-on programs, as well as test flight in general, the Air Force provided a bit of its own swagger to the enterprise. The X-15 project would, given its relatively low level of funding, be an efficient, fast-moving venture that was infused with boldness and daring. Great things happened in a short time.

SOLUTION:

Bring the parties to the table, identify their areas of strength, eliminate excessive oversight, and build a mechanism to assure a high level of cooperation.

This was a simpler program than any manned effort that NASA later attempted, which contributed to its efficiency. When the X-15 was moved around the runway, it was hauled by a truck. To test the runways out on the desert lakebeds, they would drive out there in a pickup truck and drop a steel weight to see how far it sank into the soil. It was that kind of program—if you needed a high-performance rocket engine, buy it from the best contractor you can afford and spend what it takes. But if you need a simple answer to a simple question ("Will this runway be adequate for a high-speed landing on skids?"), use the simplest and cheapest method possible: go and drop a cannonball into the dirt. It was as close to the strap-it-on-and-go rocket men of 1950s science fiction as NASA ever got.

But before any *flying* could occur, they had to actually build the thing.

INTO THE BLUE

CHALLENGE:

Design a revolutionary rocket plane on a tight budget and a constrained schedule.

The design of the rocket plane was at once innovative and derivative. The basic elements of the craft—a rocket engine, small wings, and limited control surfaces—had been partially worked out in various other aircraft, starting with German rocket-powered fighters in World War II. Other elements, such as the heat-resistant airframe and skin needed for hypersonic flight and atmospheric reentry, were new and particularly challenging.

The X-15 could experience temperatures of up to 1,200 degrees Fahrenheit (°F) with spikes of up to 1,300°F. Traditional metals such as aluminum turned to butter at these temperatures, so North American Aviation, the actual builder of the X-15, looked at other options and finally hit on a high-temperature nickel-chromium alloy called Iconel X. The material was strong and reasonably lightweight, and could stay rigid at temperatures up to 1,200°F. At higher temperatures, it would slowly deform and turn into a taffylike consistency. However, the X-15 was expected to exceed 1,200°F for only brief periods, and it was expected that between the short durations and the airframe dissipating some of the heat from affected areas, the airframe would probably be OK. *Probably.* That is how things were done in those days: you came up with your best design and tried it with a test pilot at the controls. That was their job: to test. There were no CAD designs and no software simulations. You just built it and flew. If it didn't work, you changed it and tried again. It was innovation via test-to-destruction, if necessary.

SOLUTION:

Where practical, avoid the new and exotic and use proven, reliable technologies.

The X-15 could have been designed in Hollywood—it really did look like a rocket ship. The vertical stabilizer, or rudder to us civilians, was striking, protruding just as far downward from the fuselage as it did from the top. The lower half was so long that it had to be cut loose before landing or it would hit the tarmac before the rear landing gear did.

Most of the fuselage was made up of fuel tanks, whose skin was also the outer hull of the rocket plane. A thousand gallons of liquid oxygen and 1,400 gallons of a rather nasty chemical, anhydrous ammonia, filled its belly. Forward of that were instrumentation and experiments, then the small cockpit for the pilot, tipped by a blunt nose. Behind the fuel tanks sat the rocket engine. Smaller units were used for testing, but the XLR99 engine, a massive unit with a yawning, serrated ceramic nozzle that took up the entire diameter of the rear of the plane, was the intended power plant. It could produce 60,000 pounds of thrust for a few minutes and was throttleable, a first for a U.S. rocket engine. It could propel the X-15 at a speed of 6,700 feet per second (fps)—that's about 4,500 miles per hour, or just under Mach 6. Battle tanks fire artillery shells at a velocity of about 5,500 fps. This machine was *fast.*

As the X-15 neared the apex of the flight, the engine was shut down and it coasted to its maximum altitude, as high as 345,000 feet. But at these heights, traditional control surfaces, such as flaps and ailerons, became ineffective. How the heck could you get the thing to come back into the atmosphere headed in the right direction? It could potentially come back sideways or tail-first, which would be bad.

The answer seems simple now, but was an innovative first at the time: mount small jets in the nose and wingtips that could push the front of the plane down for proper reentry into the atmosphere. Bear in mind, however, that this was 1959, and the computers and avionics that brought the space shuttle home did not exist. This was stick-and-rudder flying aided by some primitive electronics, and it could get hairy. The men who flew the X-15 earned every dollar of their pay, and then some.

> **CHALLENGE:**
>
> You never know where exactly an unpowered glider coming back from space will land.

Once the plane was into the thick atmosphere, the tiny wings went to work to allow it to glide back to its desert starting point. Perhaps "glide" is a bit of an overstatement. Another compromise in the design was the glide ratio, or the rate at which it moved forward versus the rate at which it dropped. On a recreational glider, the glide ratio might be 60:1, or 60 feet forward for every foot of descent. For a Boeing 747 it is more like 18:1—not exactly generous, but not terrible. For the X-15? It was *4:1.* For every four feet forward, it dropped a foot. This was not gliding, it was *falling.* If you fouled up your approach, there was no going around for a second try—you just dropped it wherever you were. Talk about boldness in innovation—there's nothing like the desert pavement rushing up to meet you to make one feel daring.

> **SOLUTION:**
>
> Keep it simple! Use the world's largest runways—the huge dry lake beds of Nevada and California.

As the X-15 neared the runway, it would still be traveling at between 160 and 200 mph, a speed that could destroy tires upon touchdown—so how to land the plane? The solution was a blend of innovation and simplicity. The forward landing gear, which reached the runway later than the rear units, used rubber tires (which were unsteerable in order to save weight and reduce complexity). But in back, two short struts ended in *skids*. Upon landing, the X-15 would come to a stop after one or two miles of sliding on toasty metal skis. All missions ended on the vast dry lake beds spanning California and Nevada, allowing the machine lots of room to slide out after touchdown. This allowed for unexpected changes in the flight plan when coming home from space—important when even an extra second of boost could result in a miles-long overshoot at landing.

"OK, JOE . . . 3, 2, 1 . . . LAUNCH"

Engle heard the B-52's jet engines above the sound of air rushing past the hull. Even at 45,000 feet, there was enough atmosphere out there to make quite a racket in so small a cockpit. There was no shortage of sensations when flying the X-15.

The in-flight checklist prompted him to start the engine chill-down. If one didn't run a trickle of raw liquid oxygen through the system before firing it up, the fuel in the lines could boil, the turbine could run wild, and then, *bang!* No more Joe Engle. Checklists were good things.

The guys in the bomber were ready, and the chase plane that was visible to his right concurred. He set the "igniter/idle" switch to "igniter." Engle now had 30 seconds to initiate the drop and fire up the engine or abort. The igniters in the engine were just little spark plugs, three of them, but once they were active, they were fed a stream of priming fuel and shot jets of hot flame into the combustion chamber of the rocket engine. If these little torches were left running for more than half a minute without the main rocket firing up, the engine would overheat and be damaged. There were lots of potential crisis points like that in X-planes; it was part of what made them so . . . *interesting* . . . to fly.

Engle hit the drop switch, and his stomach lurched up to meet his tonsils. He quickly ran the throttle up to 50 percent, as the engine didn't like settings below 40 percent and ran unevenly or just quit if you tried to go lower. He pulled back on the controls and throttled up, now flying almost vertically, and aimed for a point in the sky.

This was where it got tricky. There were specific target goals for each flight, and today he was aiming for about 280,000 feet. Sometimes things worked out that simply, but usually not. Running the engine a second or two too long could result in overshooting the planned altitude by 10,000 or 15,000 feet; that also meant that when you reentered and headed back to the planned landing zone, you'd come in long and might have to do some fancy flying to make it to a lakebed. A couple of the guys—including one Neil Armstrong—had overshot badly and crossed into Los Angeles airspace, flying over Pasadena's Rose Bowl before getting turned around. Engle would not let that happen to him.

As the X-15 shot skyward, the fuselage heated and expanded. The whole airframe would grow as much as two inches in length from heat expansion. Of course you could not see that from inside, but you could certainly hear the groans, bangs, and pops as the thing flexed and grew. You might also notice the smoke that sometimes filled the cockpit. It was rarely enough to interfere with flying the machine, but it got your attention.

When it was time to shut down, there was no computer or fancy automatic device to do so. There was a stopwatch on the console ahead of him, and at the right moment, he would toggle the engine off. It was not easy with as much as four times normal gravity pushing you back into the seat, but that's what test pilots got paid for. It was not supposed to be a Learjet.

Suddenly it was quiet as the rocket plane coasted another 135,000 feet toward the apogee of the flight. It was already out of most of the atmosphere, and there was no sound or real sense of motion, just a slow twist outside as the craft slowly changed orientation. Engle would soon be weightless for a few moments, and this was his chance to do a bit of sightseeing. Off to his right, he could see San Francisco Bay, surrounded by the curved terminator of the Earth. Some pilots had claimed to see as far as Seattle, but he hadn't. Regardless, the view was amazing. He didn't give a damn about the official numbers on where space started or didn't (some of the guys got pretty worked up about that)—he just loved being here. As it turned out, Engle would be one of the few X-15 pilots to receive astronauts' wings from the Air Force anyway. Funny how things worked out.

Three X-15s were built. One blew up during ground testing (with a pilot inside), but was repaired at North American (amazingly, the pilot was blown clear and survived). Another was damaged when the engine failed to function properly in flight. Aborting the flight, the pilot started to dump his fuel for an emergency landing but was unsuccessful. That X-15 came in heavy and "hot"; one of the skids collapsed, and the craft began to tumble across the lake bed. Again, the pilot survived.

CHALLENGE:

How to keep accidents and death from unnecessarily impeding a flight-test program.

A 1967 flight resulted in the only death of a pilot, when the craft experienced a hypersonic spin as it reentered the atmosphere. It broke up at 60,000 feet, spreading wreckage for almost 50 miles. The program soldiered on with two rocket planes. The X-15 never allowed anyone involved to forget that it was a high-performance plane, pushing the limits of flight, and that the mission was dangerous.

SOLUTION:

One advantage of both the military connection and little congressional oversight was that when an accident occurred, the program management could investigate, evaluate, and correct problems internally, without the public drama of congressional investigations.

JUST ANOTHER DAY IN THE COCKPIT

As the rocket plane coasted "over the top," Engle fired the thrusters on the nose to pitch it down to the proper attitude for reentry. Things got busy again. After carefully steering the craft back into the Earth's atmosphere, he would have to make the transition from using the left-hand controller, which actuated the gas thrusters, to using the right-hand controller, which operated the traditional aerodynamic controls—rudder, ailerons, and so forth. There was a control stick between his knees that would also operate the aerodynamic controls, but it was a point of pride that the pilots not use the center stick. He would fly this beast back from space using the right-hand controller, just as he always did.

So far, it had been a piece of cake. On a previous flight, an electronic control system, part of what made it possible for the X-15 to reenter without breaking up, had failed shortly after he dropped from the B-52. Engle made laconic mention of it on the radio (he might have been discussing the weather—why get all worked up?) and cycled the switch, and it eventually reengaged. Then it failed again, and he cycled it again. Flight rules called for an abort at this point, but since it was working (sort of), he figured it was OK to continue. By the time he reached his maximum altitude, it had failed 11 more times, and he had flown with one hand on the reset switch and the other on the controls. By the time he slid to a dusty stop, the unit had failed 21 times. He barely mentioned it in the postflight briefing. So far, this flight had enjoyed none of that kind of drama.

Engle came in via the usual route for a high-altitude flight. There were well-established glide routes to follow, one set for altitude flights and another for speed runs. The trick was to bring the X-15 down in the area you intended to, and he was not about to overshoot . . . the guys would never let him hear the end of it.

Not long before, in his first flight of the plane, Engle had stunned his superiors when he performed a barrel roll during his approach. He was not trying to be fancy; he was trying to scrub off excess speed and energy, and the X-15 stalled easily if you got too pushy with the angle of attack. It made sense at the time. It was a week before the maneuver was noticed when a stunned superior watched the onboard film from the flight. Engel got a brief grilling, and when he explained that he had needed to lose some speed, the bosses—all former pilots—sympathized, but asked him to please not do it again. If he did, *everyone* would want to.

Engle chuckled as he lined up his approach. Damn right they would all want to.

After a couple of figure-eight turns he was on the right heading. Everything checked out on his instrumentation, and his chase plane agreed, noting that the lower rudder had dropped off at the proper time. He came in as slowly as you could in a 15,000-pound glider that fell little more gracefully than a rock. He was unable to see the ground below him as he made his final approach; it was one of the design trade-offs. His chase plane kept him apprised of his final closing altitude. These were heights where a slightly inaccurate altimeter could cause you a bit of heartburn.

Just a few feet above the desert pavement he dropped the nose and deployed the landing gear. The rear skids hit the desert with a thud, then the craft pivoted down and the nose wheel made contact. The plane slid for two miles before it halted. By the time he had the canopy open, he was surrounded by the rescue and retrieval vehicles and a large cloud of dust. Just another day in the cockpit.

The X-15 flew higher and faster than any winged aircraft before or since. It pioneered technologies that were used in the space shuttle, which Engle also flew during its testing phase. The X-15 flew 199 times and suffered only a single pilot fatality. The program spanned 11 years, generating results that would not be matched until the space shuttle flew 12 years later.

INNOVATIONS

- Developed the first rocket plane ever built and flown.
- Developed the first use of maneuvering thrusters in space.
- Pioneered the use of advanced alloys in aircraft/spacecraft construction.
- Pioneered methods of reentering Earth's atmosphere.
- Initiated a successful cooperative partnership between the U.S. Air Force, the U.S. Navy, and NASA, a civilian agency.
- Developed pressure suits that would later be adapted for use in space.
- Explored the realm of hypersonic flight and demonstrated characteristics of winged craft at these speeds, data that were later utilized for both the space shuttle and various high-speed military aircraft.

CHAPTER 4

FIRST TO MARS: *MARINER 4*

CHALLENGES

- Design, launch, and navigate the first interplanetary probe to Mars.
- Discover how to power a tiny spacecraft with very little heat or light.
- Envision and prepare for worst-case unknowns, such as meteor swarms and radiation, with little experience in robotic spaceflight.
- Command and control a spacecraft from as far as 80 million miles away.
- Design, build, and operate the first TV camera sent to another planet.

MEETING THE GOD OF WAR

In early 1965, Mars seemed about as far away as it had for the previous 6,000 years. Since that time, when the Egyptians started chronicling the blood-red star and its odd motions in the sky, Mars has held a special fascination for every culture. Because of its color, it was always associated with fire, blood, and war. In short, the place had a lousy reputation.

In the late 1950s and early 1960s, scientists first began to think seriously about sending a robot off to take a closer look. Since the 1700s, large telescopes had revealed increasingly intriguing views of the Red Planet: dark expanses would come and go, blocking out parts of the ruddy disk. But even into the mid-twentieth century, telescopic views swam into and out of focus because of the constantly moving atmosphere on Earth. It was hard to get a good look at Mars.

Just four years after NASA had struggled to loft an 30-pound satellite into Earth orbit, the space agency had flown the world's first successful interplanetary probe past Venus, *Mariner 2* (the Soviet Union had tried for Venus and failed a year earlier). Literally blind as a bat (all it could "see" with was an infrared sensor), the machine carried little more than a radio, light sensors, and a simple radiation measuring instrument, but it was a start. Now, buoyed by this success, NASA aimed for Mars. *Mariners 3* and *4* would attempt to fly past that planet, measuring radiation and a variety of other natural phenomena in a way similar to the Venus mission (*Mariner 3*, however, failed shortly after launch.).

Since the beginning, the Jet Propulsion Laboratory has been ground zero for America's robotic missions into space. The lab is funded by NASA, but in an arrangement unique to NASA field centers, it is managed by the California Institute of Technology, or Caltech. The lab had been started by the university in the late 1930s to explore propulsion technologies and was then taken over by the U.S. Army in 1943 as part of the war effort. In 1958, the lab was merged with NASA. But all along, Caltech was running the show, and this provided a unique environment and management structure: it was, and is, the only NASA center operated by, and like, a university. The JPL "campus," as it is referred to, could be mistaken for an academic institution, and the resemblance is more than skin-deep.

Most of the top minds here are professors at Caltech or other institutions of higher learning, and the administrative structure—while certainly bureaucratic enough to please NASA—has an academic bent as well. This has been, arguably, one reason that JPL has been so consistently successful, decade after decade.

This university connection gave JPL access to some of the finest minds in the space science and astronomy field, and one such mind was that of Dr. Robert Leighton.

Leighton had become a professor of physics at Caltech in 1949, but his lifelong passion was telescopes and astronomy. When he was apprised of NASA's interest in funding a mission to Mars, he made it known that he thought the dollars could be better used to build three or four more Palomar-sized telescopes, with enough money left over to buy the mountains they would sit on. But NASA was insistent on its mission and invited him to join the project. Never one to miss an adventure, Leighton reluctantly agreed.

THE EYES OF MARINER

Right up front, he knew that something was wrong with the mission. It was designed to do great science as it whizzed past the planet—this was a flyby, not an orbital mission—but that was not enough. Yes, the spacecraft would measure radiation, take spectroscopic observations, measure atmospheric density, and fulfill a host of other useful and exciting science goals. But, would it capture the hearts and

CHALLENGE:

Maximize scientific returns from a Mars probe while engaging the public mind.

minds of the American citizens who had provided the dollars to pay for it? Leighton thought not, but he had an idea: pictures.

As it turned out, a number of other scientists on the mission had also felt the need for a photographic peek at Mars as the craft conducted its other work. But how, in an age where film was still very slow and had to be developed in bulky metal tanks full of chemicals, could you accomplish such a thing—especially in zero-G?

And then it came to them: television.

The medium of television was still young in those years, and the cameras used to capture shows like the *Ed Sullivan Show* were as big as a lawn tractor. Still, the idea seemed promising, if only they could figure out a way to achieve it.

Besides the scientific reasons for seeing the surface of Mars close up, there was a more whimsical one. People wanted to *see* Mars. Since the 1870s, astronomers like Giovanni Schiaparelli and Percival Lowell had been hand-drawing maps of the planet, covered with linear canals and dark areas that were generally thought of as oceans or forests. With these fuzzy telescopic interpretations, some people, especially Lowell, had come to believe that these lines, or canals as they were now known, must be the work of intelligent beings on the planet. How else could straight lines exist? And so many? Lowell invented a whimsical Martian empire full of planet-girdling engineering marvels, with the canals being designed to bring water from the icy polar caps to the thirsty, dying equatorial regions of the planet.

Since Lowell's ideas peaked in popularity (and they were indeed popular), other observations of Mars had begun to cast doubt on his thesis. The atmosphere was far thinner than had been thought, its composition was far more hostile, and the lack of any measurable moisture seemed to point in another direction. However, the astronomers could not prove that he was entirely wrong. Humanity needed a closer look to know once and for all whether a sister civilization lived nearby, or whether Mars was just another lifeless hunk of rock.

Besides all this, Leighton felt a nagging sense that people would just want to see the planet. Data are fine, research results are wonderful, but there is nothing quite as profound as seeing another world with your own eyes. And after years of looking at Mars and lots of other celestial targets through some of the world's best telescopes, he was ready for a close-in view.

SOLUTION:

Fly the first-ever TV camera in deep space and give the public something to see—a pathway to hearts, minds, and continued funding.

The state of the art in TV, as mentioned, did not lend itself to portability, much less flying on a small spacecraft. The main body of the *Mariner 4* probe was only about four feet wide by less than two feet high. To put it in perspective, the entire body of the spacecraft was about the size of two or TV cameras of the age. And of course, this structure had to contain not just the camera (which was a bit of an afterthought, after all), but propulsion and navigation equipment, the radio transmitter and receiver, all the scientific instruments, and the power supply. Space and weight were at a premium.

The solution that Leighton and his teammates came up with was to strip the camera to a minimum, basically building a small telescope and fastening a low-resolution video tube to the end of it. In between were a basic shutter and a couple of filters to enhance the grainy black-and-white image.

FINDING MARS

Of course, there were other parts of the mission that required the combined genius of all those involved to get them right. After all, nobody had flown to Mars before; in fact, only one planetary flyby, the mission to Venus, had been pulled off. And that planet was a lot easier to reach than Mars. How do you navigate so far from

Earth? The distance between Earth and Mars ranges from 35 to 250 million miles, and *Mariner 4* would have to cover even more distance, as the flight path was not a straight line, but a wide arc between the two worlds. And all that time, in an age when even basic computers needed a moving truck to haul them around, the probe would need to know where Earth was, where Mars was, and where it was in relation to both. It was a tricky, vexing problem.

CHALLENGE:

Navigate to Mars with minimal onboard hardware and 1960s technology.

Their solution was a model of simplicity, and it worked. They built a little photocell in a tube, a primitive version of the sensor that darkens and lightens your laptop or cellphone screen depending on the ambient light. That photocell would aim at a known star and serve to guide the probe much as ancient mariners navigated the seas via the starry skies. In this case, one photocell would find the sun (smaller and much dimmer out by Mars), then a second would search for the star Canopus. Once these two known objects were found, the spacecraft could use internal gyroscopes and thrusters to keep them firmly in view, always knowing where it was in relation to Earth and Mars. This, at least, was the theory. In practice, it was a bit harder.

Finding the sun was easy—even at this distance, it was relatively big and bright. But when they went looking for Canopus, the sensor kept locking onto other stars—or something. After a lot of head-scratching, they realized that dust and dirt had drifted out of Mariner's carcass. The star tracker was locking on to these particles instead of stars! That close in, a speck of dirt, when illuminated by the sun, looked just like a faraway star. The bigger problem was that whatever little bits of dirt and grime floated off the spacecraft continued to travel at the same speed as the probe, because there was no atmosphere in space to slow them down. Hence there was a little constellation of crud floating around *Mariner 4*. It took a lot of fiddling and testing to find a solution and relay it to the spacecraft. But they did, and finally the tracker found Canopus and stayed with the star most of the time.

SOLUTION:

Use simple, basic technology to track bright stars with known locations.

When all was said and done, the navigation scheme worked brilliantly. As the team members worked through the early challenges, they learned one valuable lesson that would help during future missions: when a problem develops, come up with a solution, then test the heck out of it on a ground-based twin of the spacecraft before sending the commands skyward for execution. The few times in JPL's history where it has tried to skimp on this step by not thoroughly testing on ground-based units or software simulators first, the results have not been good. In one case, it resulted in a spacecraft crashing into Mars; in another, it caused a lander to reorient its radio dish away from Earth, ending the mission. So extensive testing has become standard operating procedure. This intricate dance between ground-based computing and testing, along with increasing on-board capabilities, would lay the groundwork for all JPL interplanetary flights for the next 50 years.

GOODBYE, MARTIANS . . . HELLO, MARS

On July 14, *Mariner 4* flew past Mars at a closest distance of about 6,000 miles. It snapped 22 photos, recording them on 380 feet of magnetic tape. After the probe cleared Mars, it sent those images back ever so slowly: it took hours for each tiny 200-pixel by 200-line shot to reach JPL.

CHALLENGE:

Computers were slow in 1965, and we wanted to see the pictures *now*.

As the data crawled in, the excited project scientists at JPL and Caltech simply could not wait for the slow computers of the day to assemble the photos. In a flash of inspiration, one of them mounted the numeric printout of the first Mars image, which was simply rows of black numbers on printer paper, on an office wall. He made a quick trip to a local art store, looking for grayscale chalk; the snobbish clerk instead sent him back with an overpriced box of flesh-toned artist's pastels. After making careful note of numeric color values, he colored in the numbers to provide an approximation of the first look at Mars. The resulting drawing was compelling; however, the orange and yellow tones—which turned out to be fairly close to real Mars colors—were coincidental. The scientist had been looking for grayscale equivalents, and it had been a toss-up between red and yellow or purple and green.

The drawing is the only surviving *Mariner 4* image in color, and it still hangs in a place of honor at JPL.

SOLUTION:

Paint by the numbers! Print out a numeric representation of light and dark areas, then fill it in with crayons. *Inspired and simple.*

After a few days of data processing, the actual black-and-white images were printed out. The results were stunning. Before them spread a desolate, cratered landscape. Of course, most of the people involved with the mission had expected these features, but it was still shocking just how much like our own moon Mars looked. There were no canals, no vegetation, no oceans. Even at the low 1-kilometer resolution of the primitive camera, it was clear: Lowell's Martian empire was smashed to red dust.

But with that, a new Mars swam into view. Some of the landforms, fuzzy and indistinct though they might be, looked odd. Later Mariner flights revealed that they were worn in interesting ways . . . some of them reminiscent of a water-eroded landscape. That was a game-changer.

In his office some months later, Leighton reflected on the mission and the shock that his camera had sent through humanity. It was all a bit humbling. On the one hand, he felt that while the results of the mission were thrilling, the images were of limited scientific value, and that bothered him. It had been expensive, on the order of $150 million in 1965 dollars. He felt that a lot of telescopes could have been bought with that money, and more data might have been gleaned from them than from this all-too-brief flyby. But there were other voices who felt differently, and one letter in particular stuck in his mind even years later. A milkman living in Oregon had written to him, saying in awestruck tones: "I'm not very close to your world, but I really appreciate what you are doing. Keep it going." As Leighton later put it, "A letter from a milkman . . . I thought that was kind of nice." He was a modest man.

Regardless of Leighton's personal feelings, the world's first space-capable camera had flown to another planet and set the tone for all future planetary exploration; ultimately, it influenced the decision to send TV cameras along to the Apollo moon landings. In the process, Leighton brought the wonders of space closer to humanity, which is, after all, what exploration is ultimately all about.

INNOVATIONS

- A compact and robust spacecraft chassis and electronic design, capable of withstanding radiation, micrometeor impacts, and enormous changes in temperature.
- The first TV camera capable of traveling across space to image another world.
- Data recording and playback techniques to allow storage and transmission of the images and data received in delayed time.
- Command and control for a machine up to 80 million miles away, with a very short primary mission and a critical time window.
- Designing and testing the complex flight software required to navigate to Mars using the earliest computers.

CHAPTER 5

SWIMMING IN SPACE

CHALLENGES

- Train astronauts who are used to living and working on Earth how to do both in the weightless environment of space (extravehicular activity, or EVA).
- As part of this, develop ground-based EVA simulations that convincingly mimic weightlessness.
- Develop EVA-capable spacesuits, tools, and techniques to allow technical tasks to be accomplished in weightlessness.
- Develop and evolve in-house management tools to support the needed task of creating EVA procedures.

HOW HARD CAN IT BE?

It was going to be a cakewalk. Just depressurize the capsule, open the hatch, slowly stand up, and drift out into the great unknown. A few puffs of the a handheld gas jet to stabilize and reposition yourself, enjoy the view a bit, then slip back into the Gemini capsule. Easy.

At least, that was the general idea. Ed White was about to fly on *Gemini 4*, only the second flight of the new spacecraft. Gemini was the follow-on to America's first foray into space, Project Mercury. But Gemini was far more ambitious: it held two astronauts instead of one, was highly maneuverable, and could dock with other spacecraft. It was the final proving ground for operations that were critical for Apollo and the moon missions.

White was also scheduled to become the first American to walk in space. The Soviets had accomplished that feat in March of that same year, another embarrassing win in the space race. It seemed that the United States was always just a few months, or sometimes even just weeks, behind the Russians in everything to do with space. But Alexi Leonov had performed the first extravehicular activity in history, and now NASA had to catch up—again.

America knew that it had been beaten. What was not known at the time, because of the closed, secretive nature of Soviet media, was just how close to becoming a permanent satellite Leonov had been. After opening the hatch of the tiny Voskhod capsule, he adjusted the pressure in his space suit and emerged into open space, drifting near the capsule for 24 minutes and enjoying the experience immensely.

But a pressure suit is basically a balloon. When you are sitting inside the capsule's pressurized cabin, the suit is just that—a suit. When you travel into a vacuum, such as during an EVA, however, the suit must be inflated to at least 3.5 pounds per square inch (psi) to keep you alive. Even at that low pressure, the suit inflates and stiffens like crazy, leaving the astronaut looking—and feeling—somewhat like an immobilized Michelin Man. And this was 1965, when space suits were still in their infancy, modeled after fighter pilots' high-altitude pressure suits. Very little was known about actually trying to *do* something—like moving around—in a hard vacuum.

As Leonov prepared to reenter the Voskhod capsule, he soon realized to his alarm that he was too puffed up to fit into the airlock. It was a miscalculation on the part of the designers that almost cost him his life. He had to bleed pressure out of the suit by opening a relief valve—always a tricky proposition in space—and by the time he had deflated it enough to fit back inside, the suit was no longer able to sustain him. Had it taken much longer, between the low pressure and the exertions of squeezing back into the ship, he could easily have died right there, hanging by a tether to the eighth Soviet spaceship to circle the globe. His body would have burned up when the spacecraft reentered, hanging for a time by a rapidly charring umbilical. Fortunately for him, and the Soviet space program, he managed to crawl back inside just in time.

But in May of 1965, as White and fellow *Gemini 4* crewman Jim McDivitt prepared for their mission, neither they nor NASA knew of these developments. What they did know was that walking in space could be dangerous and had to be approached with the utmost caution. And what only McDivitt knew shortly before the mission, when he got a final—and private—briefing before the flight, was that if something went wrong during the spacewalk and White was unable to get back inside the capsule, he was to cut White's umbilical air line, and close the hatch, aborting the mission and coming home alone. There was no way he could help his crewmate if he were injured, sick, or otherwise incapacitated. He was not looking forward to that possibility.

Indeed, many things could have gone wrong. White could have become too disoriented and tired to jam himself back into the Gemini capsule. He could have gotten space sickness, a problem that cropped up later in the program, vomited inside his helmet, and effectively choked to death. Or he could have sprung a fatal leak in his suit (they were only rubber bladders surrounded by nylon fabric, after all). Or . . . or . . . .

McDivitt and White put these thoughts out of their minds as the Titan rocket hurled them into orbit on June 3. After a few revolutions, shortly after passing over Hawaii the third time, they depressurized the cabin and White opened his hatch. Slowly he rose out of the tiny capsule, paused to stand and assess things, then floated free, attached only by his umbilical. He had a small gas-thruster gun that he used to maneuver a bit, and he was having the time of his life. Too much so, in fact. It took repeated and increasingly strident messages from flight director Chris Kraft to bring him back inside; after 36 minutes, White reluctantly lowered himself back inside and closed the hatch. But the spacewalk was a success, and it appeared that we would soon surpass the Soviets by doing actual work in space.

How hard could it be?

Two goals of the Gemini program were critical to Apollo: rendezvous in space and EVAs, that is, astronauts leaving the spacecraft while it was in space and doing work while floating outside. NASA management had put a great deal of work into the former, but, as those involved soon realized, not enough into the latter. EVA would suddenly turn into a thorny problem. And with launches about every 10 weeks, solutions needed to be found quickly.

CHALLENGE:

How to actually perform work in space wearing a bulky, stiff pressure suit.

The next few flights were occupied with trying to rendezvous with a rocket stage called an Agena that was launched shortly before the Gemini capsule. The problem was that the Agenas kept blowing up or failing once they were in space. It was *Gemini 9* before NASA could attempt another spacewalk, but this one was to be a doozie, a real showstopper. At least, that was the plan.

The crew was made up of Tom Stafford and Gene Cernan. Cernan had been training for his EVA for months. It was ambitious: he would exit the capsule, move via small handholds to the rear cowling, perform some basic tasks, and then don an Air Force–designed jetpack. Considering that this was NASA's second attempted spacewalk, it was a bold plan.

SOLUTION:

Test "spacewalking" (performing actual tasks in a weightless, airless environment) with a series of space flights.

Cernan was optimistic: White's EVA had gone off easily, and what White could do, Cernan could do better. But White had been *adrift* in space . . . tethered to the capsule and maneuvering with his gas gun, with little more to accomplish than to prove that it could be done. For this flight, Cernan would have to do work in space—experiment with tools, climb to the back of the capsule, don the jetpack, and so forth. It would turn out to be a tall order.

It's important to remember that in space, a body is truly free—free to drift, and free to spin out of control at the slightest misstep or provocation. Even subtle motions (such as the movement of an arm or a slightly uneven push-off from a spacecraft) could send an astronaut tumbling. Magnify this by the intense effort required to turn a wrench on a bolt (which ends up spinning the astronaut and not the bolt), and you are in uncharted territory. It was new, it was bizarre, and it turned out to be nearly impossible.

The mission began with the attempted launch of an Agena stage to serve as a rendezvous target. In what could have been construed as a bad sign, the thing exploded on its way up. It was hastily replaced with a less-complex device, on another Titan, that would be a passive target.

The Titan lofted them into space flawlessly, but once they were there, they realized that the Agena's replacement was compromised and had not deployed properly. Apparently, fate did not intend to allow a rendezvous in *Gemini 9*. They moved on to the planned EVA.

Cernan ventured out and immediately began to tumble. Regaining control with extreme effort, he started the laborious process of moving hand-over-hand to the rear of the capsule. But the stiff, inflated suit made it backbreaking work; Cernan characterized it as "like working inside a suit of rusty armor." Eventually he reached the rear of the capsule and inserted his feet into a restraint there, but by now his pulse rate had skyrocketed because of the effort of fighting the pressure suit in order to move. Worse still, his exertions had overpowered the spacesuit's modest cooling system, and his faceplate was fogged over. He had to rub his nose against the plastic to make a small spot to see through. But tired and blind though he was, he was still ready to try the AMU rocket pack when a command came up from Houston: give it up. Reluctantly, Cernan returned to the cockpit, panting and exhausted. He had trouble getting back inside the cramped spacecraft, and by the time they got the hatch closed, his visor was so fogged that Stafford could not see his face at all. They completed the mission and came home three days after they had left. It had been a close thing.

CHALLENGE:

Working in space is much harder than anticipated.

"WE HAVE A LOT TO LEARN ABOUT EVA"

Once again, a productive EVA had eluded them. Chris Kraft, who was in charge of things at Houston, later lamented, "How could we have been so dumb?" It was clear that working in space was going to take much more attention. Kraft realized that he and program management had given insufficient attention to training for EVA; there had just been so much else to do.

But EVA was a critical part of the Apollo moon missions. If there were an emergency in space—say a jammed hatch between the capsule and the lunar lander—they would have to be prepared to perform an EVA between the two craft. They simply had to get this right.

The next Gemini flight, number 10, was coming up fast. John Young would command, with Mike Collins (later the Command Module pilot for *Apollo 11*) in the second seat. Collins had a pair of scheduled EVAs, each with ambitious goals. There was not much time to prepare.

On July 18, 1966, *Gemini 10* roared out of the Cape, docking with an Agena that had actually made it into orbit. On the 19th, Collins performed what was called a "stand-up EVA": open the hatch, stand on the seat with the upper two-thirds of his suited body outside, and take pictures. Even so, by the time he was done and back inside the ship, he was dog-tired.

A day later, still docked to the Agena stage, Collins began the second EVA. His first task was to retrieve an experiment from the Gemini capsule, which he did, but like Cernan before him, only with great difficulty and exertion. But far more was in the playbook.

He maneuvered to the Agena to pick up another experiment, but found that its sides were too smooth to offer a good grip. He finally located an exposed bundle of wires that he could clutch and made his way to the experiment package, but it was exhausting. Besides everything else, his umbilical, a stiff collection of air hoses, wires, and cable, got coiled up around his legs. John Young made the wise decision to call off the rest of the EVA. But even Collins's return to the capsule was less than graceful, as Young had to work feverishly to gather up a few dozen yards of stiff, bulky umbilical hose so that he could come back inside. Once again, by the time he got in and buttoned up the hatch, Collins was exhausted.

There had to be a better way. NASA management had given EVA short shrift, but Buzz Aldrin, awaiting his turn in *Gemini 12*, had been pondering the problem from the sidelines. He was certain that he knew what to do.

SOLUTION:

Develop a training regimen that simulates, as realistically as possible, weightless conditions.

ZERO-G ON A BUDGET

Since the Mercury days, training had been recognized as a critical part of spaceflight. And the problem of zero-g training was particularly sticky. They tried cable rigs with pulleys and weights, but it was unconvincing. They built metal chairs on air bearings (that worked like Air Hockey tables), but that was good only for gross movements in two dimensions. They eventually converted an Air Force KC-135 (the military version of the Boeing 707) into a flying zero-g simulator and flew parabolic arcs with it. The astronauts could ride in the back, and, much as on a roller coaster, as they dived downward, everyone who was not strapped down became weightless. It was the best simulation of all, but it was limited to a few minutes at best, and some people found it uncomfortable. It earned the nickname "Vomit Comet" for a good reason.

CHALLENGE:

Simulating weightlessness on Earth.

Finally, in 1964, a team from NASA's Langley Research Center began to look into underwater training. Those involved felt that it was the best way to create a simulated weightless condition with three axes of motion. They would put a man in a pressure suit and ballast it with lead weights until it and the man it enclosed were neutrally buoyant. Then the trainee would practice EVA tasks for as long as he needed to, often for hours. It became the most useful simulation of all. The problem was getting people to use it.

In the rough-and-ready days of Gemini, neither the funds nor the time were available to build the multimillion-gallon tank that NASA now uses for such simulations. Instead, the small team of engineers rented a pool from the McDonough Boys Military Academy in Baltimore. They paid the same rate as the Red Cross did for training lifeguards, and they had to promise not to interfere with swim meets at the school. But it was the best they could do.

The people responsible for training the Gemini astronauts came to look and were largely unimpressed. The "Old Heads," the original Mercury astronauts, thought it was silly. The manager of the Gemini program, Kenneth Kleinknecht, went so far as to say that such training was "beneath the dignity of an astronaut." Many people agreed with him.

But Aldrin (who was himself a scuba diver) disagreed. He knew that it would be helpful for learning how to accomplish complex activities in zero-g. So he set out, quietly at first, to convince the brass at the Manned Spaceflight Center in Houston. He and Scott Carpenter, a Mercury astronaut, spoke to anyone who would listen about the efficacy of neutral-buoyancy simulation. They faced a tough audience.

SOLUTION:

Train with appropriate tools and restraints in water—an almost frictionless environment.

After much campaigning, a partial Gemini simulator was lowered into the pool at the boys school. Gene Cernan, who had been defeated by his own spacewalk attempt in *Gemini 9*, suited up and tried his hand in the pool. He came out both frustrated and relieved—the former because he too found it hard to get much done with the tools at hand; the latter because he could finally stop blaming himself for his foiled attempts on his own flight.

It was not the astronaut who was to blame, but a lack of preparation. Cernan, also a diver, was convinced.

CONVINCING NASA

Aldrin continued to lobby hard for time in the water, but Alan Shepard, America's first man in space and the head of the astronaut office, would not hear of it. It was *unmanly*. It took a direct order from the top brass to get Shepard to relent, and he did so grudgingly. But Aldrin didn't care—he was determined to get it right on his flight, the last of the Gemini series.

Meanwhile, the unstoppable juggernaut known as the flight schedule soon sent *Gemini 11* into orbit, with Pete Conrad commanding and Dick Gordon set to perform his own EVA. Surely this time they would meet with success. Both were supremely confident (of course, being astronauts in the 1960s, they were always supremely confident) and felt ready to tackle the challenge.

Prior to launch, a test engineer at the pool had performed, and filmed, close to 50 hours of underwater training, and much of it pertained to this flight. The footage was rushed to Houston, where it was, apparently, immediately ignored. It seemed that the prejudice against floating around in a high school pool was not gone yet. Both the astronaut corps and NASA management had not yet embraced the need for extensive preflight EVA training. As before, it would cost them dearly.

> **CHALLENGE:**
>
> Convince management and coworkers to accept an unorthodox solution.

But Aldrin was undeterred. Even as *Gemini 11* was headed into orbit, he was doggedly practicing his own EVA in the water. The next day, as Dick Gordon struggled to accomplish a simple task in his first EVA (which was cut short after only 38 sweaty, frustrating minutes), Aldrin calmly and competently executed similar tasks in the confines of the McDonough pool. The last Gemini flight was less than two months away, and the problem of EVA still loomed large. Finally, management was becoming nervous enough to look at a workable solution. The managers were late to the game, with just a few weeks to the final Gemini mission, but they allowed Aldrin to dramatically step up his simulations in preparation for his program-ending EVA.

SOLUTION:

Belief in your idea, underscored by extensive proof of concept and a willingness to "swim upstream" against entrenched and outdated ideas.

The key was restraint—not of the temper, but of the body. One simply had to make sure that his body was anchored in the right place so that torquing motions of any kind would not send him spinning. It was critical that the astronaut be secured by at least one axis; the rest was muscle control and careful calculation of movements.

November 11 was as splendid a day as the Florida coast had to offer. *Gemini 12* vanished into the skies above Cape Canaveral. This was NASA's last chance to get it right. Back in Houston, watching on a projection screen in Mission Control, Chris Kraft had a knot in his stomach. Do or die; this was the one. They were all counting on Aldrin.

Soon Aldrin and Lovell were closing the gap between their Gemini capsule and the requisite Agena stage, which had been launched well ahead of them for rendezvous practice. Just as things were looking smooth as butter, the onboard radar failed. One minute they had a lock on the Agena, the next they did not. A groan sounded in Mission Control. Kraft knew that it was hard enough to rendezvous *with* radar; the chances of the two men completing the maneuver without it were slim.

> **CHALLENGE:**
> Completing orbital rendezvous with a broken flight navigation computer.

TRIUMPH VIA TRAINING

But he did not factor in Buzz Aldrin's obsessive nature. In addition to his extensive preparation in weightless training, Aldrin was well versed in the mechanics of orbital rendezvous from his time in the doctoral program at MIT, where his thesis had been on orbital mechanics—so much so that the other astronauts, who were in general more of the "strap-it-on-and-go" variety, called him "Doctor Rendezvous." It was not necessarily a compliment. But today it would make all the difference.

Up in orbit, Lovell knew that if they could not mate with the Agena, most of their mission goals would not be accomplished. But just inches away, in the right-hand seat, Aldrin was unpacking the manual sextant and celestial charts. It seemed almost unreal—they were going to attempt to dock two spacecraft with tools dating from the age of sailing ships.

After a couple of orbits and intense concentration, Aldrin looked up, and there was a bump, a scraping sound, and the beautiful sound of docking latches snapping closed. They not only had found the errant Agena, but were now snugly mated to it. Crisis number one was resolved, and all through the use of what he later referred to as the "Mark I cranium." And as if that were not enough to impress his skeptical colleagues 160 miles below, Lovell had used less fuel performing a manual rendezvous than some other flights had burned through using radar.

SOLUTION:

Continuous practice with traditional navigation tools—that is, sextant, slide rule, and pencil and paper— and revolutionary methods to be able to perform such maneuvers manually when necessary. In short, be prepared to step in when technology fails.

About 21 hours into the flight, it was time for the first EVA. This was the easy one: open the hatch, stand up, and acclimatize to space. For two and a half hours, Aldrin did just that, and without a hitch. This may seem like an overly long period to take pictures and sightsee, but there was more to it than that. It was important to make sure that he would not get sick outside the spacecraft. For one thing, if he vomited inside his helmet during his spacewalk (which never did happen, but plenty of astronauts got sick inside of space capsules), he would die a choking death. Then Lovell would have to use the dreaded scissors to snip Aldrin's umbilical and come home alone. Fortunately, the first EVA went perfectly. Before he returned to his seat, Aldrin installed a handrail and some handholds on the exterior of the capsule to make tomorrow's more ambitious EVA easier. NASA had learned at last, and hopes were high that this hard-earned knowledge would pay off.

The next day the pressure was on, although you would never have guessed it from Aldrin's demeanor. He and Lovell calmly went through their checklists in preparation for the second EVA. But down in Mission Control, the mood was different—this was not just the second EVA of *Gemini 12*, but the final one of the entire Gemini program. Failure to accomplish the basic goals set out for Aldrin could seriously jeopardize the plans for Apollo. As the second hands on the wall-mounted clocks in Mission Control swept closer to egress time, tension grew.

Soon Aldrin exited the spacecraft. He installed a couple of restraint devices onto his spacesuit and moved forward via the handrails. All along he kept up a running commentary on his progress, never becoming winded or sweaty, as his predecessors had. Soon he reached the Agena to which they had docked and attached items there for a later experiment. He then reversed course, hauling himself to the back of the capsule. Once there, he slipped his boots into restraints and performed chores similar to those that had defeated so many before him. This time, it all worked as planned. Aldrin tightened bolts, snipped metal, moved devices around, and made it all look easy.

Aldrin's only regret was that there had not been more to do. The Air Force had still wanted to fly their jetpack with an astronaut, but NASA would not sanction it. They just wanted a clean EVA. For his part, Aldrin would have been happy to add it to the checklist, so confident was he of his preparations.

On the way back into the capsule, he stopped and looked into his partner's window. It was covered in greasy grime, a by-product of repeated thruster firings. Aldrin took a moment to wipe the window clean, to which Lovell responded, "Hey, would you change the oil too?" It all came off as light-hearted and proficient. And while this bravura performance was the result of many factors, including data from previous spacewalk attempts, careful mission planning, and endless practice, Aldrin (enthusiastically) and most others in the program (sometimes reluctantly) had to admit one thing: the neutral-buoyancy training in the McDonough boys school pool had made all the difference. The headmaster should have been proud.

INNOVATIONS

- Early use of recreational water pools to simulate weightless conditions.
- Development of special tools and restraints for use by astronauts while training in the water and on identical units to be used in space.
- Evolution of the astronauts' dedication to training for EVAs.
- Individual effort to convince upper management of the efficacy of underwater training for EVAs.

CHAPTER 6

THE DAY NASA GREW UP: *APOLLO 1*

CHALLENGES

- How to recover, technically, emotionally, and strategically, from a tragic human loss and program setback.
- Taking responsibility and learning from mistakes to prevent future occurrences.
- Negotiating with contractors to identify and correct problems.
- Redesigning complex and expensive equipment for fire safety.
- Fair apportionment of responsibility for the accident while observing political considerations.
- Dealing with hostile forces that impeded recovery.

JUST A SIMPLE TEST . . .

Friday, January 27, 1967, was a day much like many others at the Cape. People went about their jobs, and the Kennedy Space Center hummed with activity. The primary focus was over at Pad

34, where the Saturn 1B rocket sat with the first man-rated Apollo Command Module mounted atop it. Inside was the first crew scheduled to fly the new spacecraft into orbit. Gus Grissom, the mission commander, was a veteran of both Mercury and Gemini missions, and was regarded as one of the most experienced and seasoned astronauts. Ed White, the Lunar Module pilot (although he would not have one on this flight, as it was a test of the capsule only) was another Gemini veteran and the first spacewalker. Finally, Roger Chaffee, the Command Module pilot, was a rookie who had never before flown in space. With a keen and inquisitive mind, he was the "egghead" of the crew. Between the three of them, they exemplified the best that NASA had to offer.

The trio had been sitting inside the cramped capsule for more than seven hours. On the schedule for this day was what was known as a "plugs-out" test, a routine but necessary part of qualifying the hardware. In essence, the Command Module sat atop the Saturn booster, which was unfueled and as safe as a bedpost. All wiring and connections from the ground to the capsule had been disconnected, as had most of the noncritical connections to the booster. In effect, the rocket was simulating a "flight condition," in which the only communication with the ground was by voice radio and telemetry. It was as close to flying the beast as you could get without launching.

The day had not been going well. Grissom, never a teddy bear, was getting particularly grouchy. There had been one glitch after another, delays upon delays. They were trying to simulate a countdown, but things kept getting in the way. Around 6 p.m., the latest problem was with communications. The radio reception was poor, and conversation with the ground controllers was almost impossible. As Grissom groused late in the day, "How the hell are we gonna fly to the moon if we can't talk between a few buildings?"

Mission Control was 1,000 miles away in Houston and monitoring the balky test. Upon hearing the commander's bellyaching, some controllers winced and others chuckled. Grissom was known for being irascible, and he was certainly living up to that reputation today. "Jee-sus Christ!" he spat. It was not a religious appellation.

As the test continued and the clock slowly ticked over to 5:30 p.m. in Houston—6:30 at the Cape—things had not improved, and people were getting tense. Everyone was tired and wanted things to smooth out so that they could get home in time for a late dinner.

Gene Kranz, the flight director at Houston's Manned Spacecraft Center, had left earlier in the day and was at home preparing for a night out. Kranz was a fixture at the Johnson Space Center (JSC), junior only to Chris Kraft, who was in charge of mission operations and just about everyone in Mission Control. As Kraft's deputy, Kranz was no slouch. An aerial combat veteran of Korea, he sported a severe crew cut that topped out above steely eyes. He had a powerful presence and was not just by-the-book—he had *written* the book. Literally. Early in his time at JSC, Kraft had given him the task of creating a manual of procedures for manned spaceflight. Kranz had attacked the project with fervor, and he was the go-to guy when questions arose. If there were no questions, he went to find some. Neither Kraft nor Kranz brooked any nonsense or tolerated sloppiness in any form; to say that Kranz brought military bearing and efficiency to the workplace was putting it mildly.

With the test crawling toward resolution, Kranz had decided to try to capture some semblance of normalcy out of the 70-hour weeks by taking his long-suffering wife to dinner. About 5:30, he had just finished dressing for his evening out when there was a loud knock on the front door. He thought it was the babysitter (the Kranz brood consisted of six children) and went down to let her in. He was surprised to see a fellow flight controller, Jim Hannigan, disheveled and breathless. While it was not unusual to see other employees of the Manned Spacecraft Center around the neighborhood (most of them lived in these new suburbs), to have one drop by unannounced on a workday was. Especially in such distress.

"Have you heard what happened?" Hannigan blurted out. Kranz cocked his head with a questioning stare. "They had a fire on the launchpad. They think the crew is dead!" And at that moment, Kranz's world, and that of all of NASA, collapsed. Their worst fears had been realized.

"WE'RE BURNING UP!"

It was not perceived as a dangerous test. The rocket was empty; there was no fuel in the tanks. It was sitting bolted to the launchpad on the ground in Florida, and was incapable of lighting a birthday candle, much less blasting off into space. The crew members were closed in the capsule, but that was simply to simulate flight conditions. They were just sitting there, throwing switches, reading gauges, and talking (when the radio worked) to the launch complex and to Houston. And then, at 6:31 Florida time, it happened.

There was a crackle of static in the communication circuit. A few controllers adjusted their headsets; this was not the usual static they had been hearing. Then, a cry was heard over the scratchy line: "Fire!" Controllers and engineers looked up, then at each other. Had they heard that right? Then, "We've got a fire in the cockpit!" There was no doubt now. Hearts froze. The controllers rapidly scanned their readouts looking for information, for anything. They were in Houston, 1,000 miles from the Cape. They were observers in an awful drama that was playing out on the far coast, and there was nothing they could do but listen to the horror playing out in Florida.

"We've got a bad fire—get us out! We're burning up!" The pad technicians flew into action. They were only a few feet away on the gantry, right next to the capsule atop the 230-foot-high rocket. One went for a fire extinguisher—a well-intentioned but useless gesture. Others simply ran to the capsule. As they neared it, they were able to see what the controllers in the launch complex just across the marshes of the Cape and others in Houston could not: space-suited hands clawing futilely at the hatch, visible through the glass porthole of the capsule. The intensity of the effort was weakening by the second.

Then, before anything could be done, the capsule blew apart, splitting along the side and spilling flame and smoke out of the rupture. The pad workers were knocked back, then recovered and threw themselves into the hot, choking smoke, trying desperately to get the hatch open. But it was not to be. The fire had largely died out by the time they wrenched it free *six minutes* later. What was inside when they peered in is best left to the imagination. The crew of *Apollo 1* was gone.

The launch complex was in an odd state of frenzy and stasis. Fire engines and an ambulance were dispatched, but by the time they got to the pad, there was little to do but water down the melted metal on the side of the capsule and confirm the deaths. The astronauts themselves—what was left of them—remained in the capsule for forensic examination.

In Houston, Kraft ordered the doors to Mission Control locked and all records collected. He told the controllers to immediately write down their impressions so that none of their memories of the terrible events would get lost.

Kranz screeched to a halt next to the doors of Mission Control. Once inside, he saw a grim-faced Kraft, who merely nodded acknowledgement, and then spoke briefly to John Hodge, the flight director on duty at the time of the accident. Hodge was in a daze, just barely holding it together. Others were not doing as well, sobbing softly. It was at that moment that Kranz realized how bad things were.

INTROSPECTION

Over the next 18 months, the program ground to a halt and engaged in painful self-evaluation. Many in Congress called for an external investigation, and some cynically even took advantage of the disaster to call for cancellation of the Apollo program altogether. But James Webb, the NASA administrator, would have none of that. Using his substantial political skills with President Johnson, he wrangled approval for an internal investigation—simply because nobody outside could understand the complexities of Apollo. Over the next year, the spacecraft, now a charred and melted ruin atop the Saturn rocket, was disassembled bolt by bolt, and a complete and thorough examination of all components was done. They *would* find the cause of the fire.

At Mission Control, technicians were wandering, chatting quietly in corners, and going over the same data again and again to find something—anything—that could explain the disaster. Some of them had to be ordered home for rest after 20 or 30 straight hours of frustrated, tearful examination of records and data printouts. Almost by unspoken instinct, the bulk of them headed to a local watering hole, in the best tradition of test pilots everywhere, to toast the fallen. But this was different—these men had not died in flight. They had died during a routine pad test, and Kranz knew that it was not a simple failure of a machine or of a person . . . it was a failure of the system. Something was rotten inside Apollo, and he was damned if he would let anything—even this—scuttle his beloved space program. He also felt a strong sense of personal failure and responsibility (many people did, as it turned out), and he would address this, too. Then they all went home. The weekend was sullen and pensive, and everyone involved struggled to come to grips with the crisis. Tears were shed, and many bottles of alcohol were emptied. All across Clear Lake, the suburb of Houston where most of them lived, men sat and stared out windows at nothing. Wives and children would come to the doorway, look at their beloved, and quietly wander off. There was nothing to be said.

By dawn Monday morning, Kranz was prepared to begin a course of action. This was a case of innovating through crisis, and he, along with Kraft and the others, would move through this crisis by taking responsibility, facing their failures, fixing what was broken, and finally by sheer force of will. In short, they would lead.

CHALLENGE:

Help your workforce to cope with a tragedy for which most feel some level of personal responsibility.

When he arrived at the space center, Kranz called a meeting of "his people." He felt that it was his turn to step up and set an example, and, in a sense, take some of the blame squarely on the jaw. In the Johnson Space Center auditorium, while John Hodge briefed the assembled staff, Kranz fumed just offstage. He had no notes and was not sure what he would say, but he knew what he felt: anger. Anger at his personal failure to protect the crew, and anger at NASA for allowing itself to be rushed to win the moon when its people knew that they were pushing their luck.

When Hodge finished, he stepped down, looking at his shoes as he took a seat. Kranz strode to the podium and took a military stance, steely-eyed and intense. Those who worked for him knew that something profound was about to happen.

THE KRANZ DICTUM

In the succeeding years, this impromptu speech became known as the Kranz Dictum. It was not flowery, it was not sentimental . . . but it was inspiring. He was clear and powerful, and nobody in that room would ever forget what he said.

Kranz squared his shoulders, and after a few perfunctory remarks got to the core of his speech. He spoke with economy and force, with candor and passion.

SOLUTION:

Face the tragedy squarely. Address the workforce candidly, with responsibility spread evenly across the team. Inspire your workforce with honesty and direct talk, and lead them toward a better future result.

> *Spaceflight will never tolerate carelessness, incapacity, and neglect. Somewhere, somehow, we screwed up. It could have been in design, build, or test. Whatever it was, we should have caught it. We were too gung ho about the schedule and we locked out all of the problems we saw each day in our work. Every element of the program was in trouble and so were we. The simulators were not working, Mission Control was behind in virtually every area, and the flight and test procedures changed daily. Nothing we did had any shelf life. Not one of us stood up and said, "Dammit, stop!" I don't know what Thompson's committee will find as the cause, but I know what* I *find. We are the cause! We were not ready! We did not do our job. We were rolling the dice, hoping that things would come together by launch day, when in our hearts we knew it would take a miracle. We were pushing the schedule and betting that the Cape would slip before we did.*

Nobody stirred; not a word was muttered. There was dead silence as the words sank in, because they all knew them to be true.

> *From this day forward, Flight Control will be known by two words: "Tough" and "Competent."* Tough *means we are forever accountable for what we do or what we fail to do. We will never again compromise our responsibilities. Every time we walk into Mission Control we will know what we stand for.* Competent

means we will never take anything for granted. We will never be found short in our knowledge and in our skills. Mission Control will be perfect. *When you leave this meeting today you will go to your office and the first thing you will do there is to write "Tough" and "Competent" on your blackboards. It will* never *be erased. Each day when you enter the room these words will remind you of the price paid by Grissom, White, and Chaffee. These words are the price of admission to the ranks of Mission Control.*

CHALLENGE:

Fix a rushed and overconfident program after a terrible loss; bring federal employees and offsite contractors to the table to prevent future failures.

It took the Apollo program almost 18 months to recover from the disaster. While the exact cause of the fire was never found, the overall causes—both technological and institutional—were. In brief:

- The Apollo capsule had been a mess. The construction had been rushed to meet Kennedy's deadline, and there were problems aplenty: faulty instrumentation, poorly installed wiring (there were almost 15 miles of wire inside the Command Module alone), a cooling system that leaked flammable fluids, and much more. Some of this was North American Aviation's fault, as it was the prime contractor for the Apollo spacecraft. But the astronauts had applied yards of flammable Velcro all over the interior, which had burned like mad. And part of the sloppiness of the construction was the result of incessant and unending change orders from NASA and from the astronauts themselves, sometimes several in a day, which meant that North American could never lock the design specs of the capsule—things changed all the time.

- The hatch design was dangerous. It was a clumsy, poorly designed, two-piece unit that opened inward. The logic behind this was simple: the spacecraft would be flying in a vacuum, and as the astronauts pumped up the oxygen inside the Command Module, it would push the hatch outward toward the restraining rim of the hull. In effect, it would simply fit better as the conditions got more extreme. The hatch was held in place by a perimeter of bolts that had to be removed individually with a wrench. At best, the whole assembly could be removed in about four minutes—an eternity with a fire burning at your feet. The astronauts never had a chance.
- Third, and most controversial, was the decision made by NASA years before to fly spacecraft with a pure oxygen environment in space—and testing with it on Earth. While there were good reasons for using a low-pressure oxygen environment in space, pumping oxygen up to sea-level pressures was an accident waiting to happen. But it had worked with both Mercury and Gemini, and so it was used for Apollo as well.

It was this last element that haunted them all. A spacecraft with a pure oxygen environment at five pounds per square inch (psi), or about one-third of sea-level air pressure, was more than enough to keep humans alive and happy in space. And at that pressure, while oxygen was not 100 percent safe, it was not likely to cause a fire if they were careful.

Unfortunately—and this was what tore at their insides—they had not been conducting ground tests at 5 psi. They had to keep the pressure differential between the inside of the Command Module and the outside pressure within 2 to 3 psi or the craft would literally implode. Further, it was desirable to pressurize the capsule higher than ambient pressure to check for leaks. So they had adopted the policy long ago of pumping the cabin up to about 17 psi of pure oxygen so that it would overpower the 14.5 psi of the outside air at the Cape and demonstrate a solid seal with the hatch and other seals. Again, it had worked for Mercury and Gemini.

But Mercury and Gemini had only a fraction of the complexity of the Apollo capsule. Further, the Mercury and Gemini flights were generally shorter, and extended weightlessness was less of an issue, so the astronauts had not covered their cabins with Velcro (it worked great to secure items that would otherwise float free and disappear or get in the way). And those capsules had not embodied the complexities required to travel to the moon and back.

SOLUTION:

Assess shortcomings and failures in the process. Dispatch teams to offsite contractors to troubleshoot design and manufacturing processes. Make everyone accountable, and learn from the mistakes made across the breadth of the operation.

In the end, there were many contributing factors, but the gross problem had been the high-pressure oxygen in the cabin environment. At that pressure, oxygen promotes burning. They flame-tested the Velcro in that environment, and instead of smoldering as it did at 5 psi, it exploded, showering the capsule with melted, burning plastic. The space suits, made from nylon, also melted. Wire insulation dripped away, and electrical arcs flew. In fact, in these conditions, *even solid aluminum would burn*. In short, at 17 psi, an oxygen-rich environment was a blazing inferno waiting to happen. It had just been a matter of time.

RECRIMINATION AND RECOVERY

The months of investigations and reconstructions of the events leading to the fire dragged on. Likewise, the congressional grilling of the top men in NASA—James Webb, George Low, and Robert Seamans—battered them, the agency, and the program. And while it was important to know what had happened, the politicized hearings accomplished little. NASA knew what had happened, knew how to fix it, and knew how to get back on track. Knowing how to get past the guilt and shame of the tragedy took a bit longer; escaping the clutches of men like Senator Walter Mondale, who seemed to hate Apollo and all that it stood for, was a tougher challenge.

The whole political aspect of the process drove Kranz and his teams crazy. They just wanted to investigate, find the failures, fix them, and move on. The astronauts, the ones whose lives were on the line, felt the same way: let's get on with it.

CHALLENGE:

Dealing with a person of authority who is needlessly hostile to your attempts to fix the problem.

In the midst of the congressional hearings, Mondale presented a long-forgotten memo from a senior NASA manager discussing issues with the Command Module and savaging North American Aviation. For his part, Webb had apparently never seen the memo and was caught off guard. This bit of "evidence," along with the shift to a Republican president,, contributed to Webb leaving NASA before *Apollo* flew to the moon.

Enter astronaut Frank Borman, who would soon trust North American's Apollo Command Module design to fly the *Apollo 8* mission around the moon with his crew. NASA had asked him to represent the astronauts in the hearings—the people whose lives would ride on the Apollo hardware. He was one of the heroes, a voice who could not be ignored. He had also been a close friend of Gus Grissom's. Somber, direct, and serious as a heart attack, Borman radiated authority and military bearing. He sat patiently through the hearings, and soon it was his turn:

> *You are asking us do we have confidence in the spacecraft, NASA management, our own training, and . . . our leaders. I am almost embarrassed because our answers appear to be a party line. Everything I said last week has been repeated by the people I see here today. The response we have given is the same because it is the truth. . . . We are trying to tell you that we are confident in our management, and in our engineering and in ourselves. I think the question is really: Are you confident in us?*

SOLUTION:

Recruit the best and most capable people; address the opposition with candor, honesty, and facts. Inspire changes in attitudes, and by doing so, overcome irrational pushback.

He went further. He said that not spotting the critical link between high-pressure oxygen environments and potential fire had been a "failure of the imagination." He recited a quote from Gus Grissom that had been written out well before the fire. Gus said that he knew that something would eventually happen, that spaceflight was a dangerous business, and that he hoped that NASA and the American people would stand firm and continue the exploration of space. Finally, Borman instructed the assembled politicians to stop the "witch hunt" and let them get on with flying to the moon.

And that was that.

In his office, Kranz heard the stories and enjoyed Borman's directness. It was not out of keeping with his own approach. And while they all knew that spaceflight was dangerous, that they would have technological and human failures, and that they would surely lose another man—or crew—in space, Kranz knew that he would never again be lax, even for a moment. He would set an example for his people, one that they would follow to the letter or even improve upon. He would, indeed, make Mission Control perfect.

Sometimes innovation is not technology, not machines, and not anything material. Sometimes it is a thing of the spirit, a core belief and strength. And sometimes it is gained through loss, grief, and painful self-examination. The changes in management and procedures resulting from the fire, both inside NASA and beyond, would stick for decades. Not until 1986, when the shuttle *Challenger* exploded during ascent, would the agency need to reexamine itself in such a painful and total way. When it did, the Kranz Dictum was invoked once again.

The Kranz Dictum is still in print, posted in multiple locations at various NASA centers, and Mission Control, almost 50 years later, still strives to be damned near perfect.

INNOVATIONS

- Top management found the proper tone to address the accident and help the workforce cope with feelings of loss and responsibility.
- Designed a procedure to dismantle the *Apollo 1* capsule and examine every component in detail for a cause of the fire.
- Interfaced with the contractor and developed a procedure to ensure against future faulty designs and construction.

- Redesigned major technologies within the spacecraft, including a total rethinking of hatch ("egress") design.
- Developed a program of "resident astronauts" at major contractors to ensure build quality and to lend a human face to the program, encouraging personal responsibility within the workforce.
- Dealt with intense (and at times predatory) government investigations.
- Led by example and inspiration.

CHAPTER 7

THE BUG

CHALLENGES

- Design and construct a vehicle unlike anything you or your workforce has manufactured before.
- Design and construct a vehicle that will never operate on or near Earth, but is capable of operating in a total vacuum far from home.
- Design-in 99.999 percent reliability with broadly redundant systems.
- Meet impossible and ever-changing weight restrictions.
- Innovate new materials and methods for handling them.
- Design and build with the absolute minimums in terms of structure and hardware to meet performance and safety requirements.
- Operate a program that is prototype-oriented in a company that is assembly-line-oriented.
- Finally, do all the above while designing for an environment that is largely unexplored and poorly understood at the time of contract award.

THE CALL

Four of them sat around the gray steel desk, staring quietly at the . . . *thing* . . . sitting in the center. Another six or so engineers clad in starchy white shirts, some sporting sweater-vests, others not, fidgeted in the office or the hallway. All of them had slide rules in a quickly accessible pocket; most had a sharpened draftsman's pencil behind one ear. A chill could be felt in the room, as it was mid-November in Bethpage, New York, and the heater in this part of the drafty old aircraft plant was not very ambitious.

A few of them concentrated on the little wooden model in the center of Tom Kelly's desk. The model was made of unfinished wood, about five inches tall, a ball of lathe-turned pine mounted on a wood disk. That assemblage was supported by five legs, made from *paper clips*, and on this little contraption rode the future of the Grumman Aircraft Engineering Corporation. This was the design that would win or lose the firm a $500 million contract to build the Apollo program's moon lander, the Lunar Module, later known widely as the LM.

It was 1962, and the project development team was waiting for a call from NASA announcing the winner of the bid. It was the most complex, ambitious, and also daunting component of the entire Apollo project. And to Tom Kelly, staring at the forlorn, homely little model, the most beautiful.

The phone rang, and the men started in their seats. Kelly took his time picking up the bulky black receiver. The engineers waiting nearby leaned forward with anticipation.

The call was from Joe Gavin, Kelly's superior at Grumman, who passed along a press release by NASA: the LM was Grumman's. Kelly flashed a thumbs-up to the assembled staff, then cupped the phone to his ear to finish the call as the assembled engineers tried—and failed—to contain themselves. The Grumman Corporation, one of the smallest and most conservative of America's major aircraft companies, had just entered the space age. With it came Kelly, just 33 years old, and now responsible for building the most complex and unusual flying machine in history.

INTO THE UNKNOWN

There is a wonderful saying, attributed to the original "Monkey's Paw" story first published in *Harper's Magazine* in 1902: "Be careful what you wish for, as you may receive it." When it came to the Lunar Module contract, truer words were never spoken. By any measure, the project turned out to be a roller-coaster ride that required more invention and cleverness than just about any other component of Apollo. Here was the first true spaceship, a craft that would fly only in the vacuum of space. It would also, hopefully, land two men on the surface of the moon, keep them alive for a few days, lift off when they were done exploring, and rendezvous with the Command Module orbiting above the moon at more than 3,600 miles per hour. This was hair-raising stuff in 1962, and Kelly would need all his inventive genius, and that of many of others, to see it through.

The Grumman Aircraft Corporation was known for its fighter aircraft, which included the F4F Wildcat and F6F Hellcat of World War II. Grumman's fighters were large and heavy, but very lethal. Pilots loved them, and they ruled most of the Pacific Theater. After the war, Grumman moved into jets, building a number of solid but unglamorous planes such as the A-6 Intruder. If ever a company was like the aircraft it built, Grumman was that company. *Innovation* was not the first term that sprang to mind when someone mentioned the company; *conservative, tough, reliable,* and *rugged* were. When Grumman won the contract for the LM, this corporate culture would be challenged, to say the least. Stodgy Grumman would be catapulted, for all practical purposes, into the twenty-first century.

In the center of this maelstrom was Kelly. As a boy, he was fanatical about flying, but he was only 11 years old when World War II broke out, so he was forced to indulge his aerial fantasies by building wooden airplane models. Kelly held degrees in mechanical engineering and was professorial by nature. He would need all that and more to accomplish what lay ahead.

The space age was young, and only two other airplane companies had made the jump into creating space vehicles: McDonnell-Douglas was building the recently launched Mercury capsule, and North American the X-15 rocket plane. In contrast, Grumman still built machines that flew through *air*, using wings and control surfaces such as flaps and rudders to maneuver. These were driven by air-breathing jet engines and were sleek and aerodynamic, slicing their way through the atmosphere with elegant ease. To most of the designers, their airplanes were as much objects of beauty as war machines.

But the LM would never fly in an atmosphere and never operate in a full Earth-gravity environment. It would maneuver in an airless environment using rockets and had virtually no aerodynamic surfaces. The entire ship was meant to land on the moon and return to orbit—once. It would then be discarded, so everything had to work just once. But it had to work *perfectly* . . . there was no room for error, *none*. The LM was about as far from an airplane as you could get. Kelly had his work cut out for him. To say that he would innovate his way to the moon's surface is to vastly understate the accomplishment: Tom Kelly, and the thousands of Grumman employees who ultimately worked on the project, had to reinvent the way they thought about building a flying machine. His senior engineers would say, "Look at these drawings! Just look at the shape of this silly thing! Everything sticks out . . . it's gonna break!" This was new ground that would tax them to the limit, nearly break NASA's bank account, and cause more than a few nervous breakdowns, heart attacks, alcoholic binges, and divorces. But they did it, possibly better than anyone else could have done.

UNDERSTANDING THE CHALLENGE

CHALLENGE:

Avoid design and process fixation.

To get started, the team had to interpret and then refine the goals that NASA had placed before it. While NASA had specified what the machine had to do, it was largely up to Grumman to figure out *how*:

- Take a crew of two from lunar orbit to the moon's surface.
- Carry tools, experiments, a nuclear fuel power generator, and ultimately a car with them.
- Allow them to leave the craft and explore the moon.
- Support them for up to three days to eat and sleep on the moon.
- Allow for multiple exits and entries in a dusty, vacuous, and largely unknown environment.
- Bring them back to lunar orbit and rendezvous with the Command Module.
- Do all of these things perfectly, every time, with virtually no margin for error or failure.

That's it: just take two guys to the moon and back with 100 percent reliability—at a time when we weren't even sure what the surface of the moon was made of.

Of course, NASA would be involved every step of the way—sometimes to a maddening degree. For example, there were the dreaded NASA quality control inspectors. They would crawl all over the LMs during construction, literally sandwiched between a Grumman technician and the thin wall of the spacecraft, peering over his shoulder after he installed a part, reviewing each bit of the task:

INSPECTOR: *"[Did you] place support clamp PN AN 269972 on water line PN LDW 390-22173-3 on location shown in sketch?"*

[Inspector shows technician sketch.]

TECHNICIAN: *"OK, part number AN 269972 installed on water line LDW 390-22173-3."*

INSPECTOR: *"Verify that rubber grommet on clamp is properly seated, with no metal touching the tubing."*

[Both look to see that this is the case.]

TECHNICIAN: *"OK, rubber grommet on clamp is properly seated, with no metal touching."*

INSPECTOR: *"Align holes in clamp with hole in structure PN LDW 270-13994-I."*

And so forth. This gives you some idea of the rigor, expense, and time-consuming nature of the work. A Lunar Module was not something that one just built; it was willed into being.

Kelly and his team began by questioning all existing assumptions. This may have been one of the most forward-looking moments of the entire Apollo effort, for the Lunar Module broke more new ground than any other part of the program. Kelly would "let form follow function," and with this in mind, the project began to take shape.

SOLUTION:

Let form follow function. Move past previous thinking and assumptions to design a machine for this new task and environment.

The initial design was not dissimilar to the little wood ball with paper-clip legs that had helped Grumman to win the contract. The

LM would be a two-stage lander. The bottom stage would be a squat cylindrical unit, supported by five legs. The upper stage, where the astronauts would ride, was modeled after helicopter cockpits of the time: a roughly spherical cabin with four large windows that would allow the astronauts a sweeping view of the moon's surface as they made the dangerous journey downward. There would be docking hatches front and top, and the whole thing looked purposeful and futuristic.

The design made sense from an aircraft designer's perspective, but it was absolutely unworkable from Kelly's. The principal problem was weight. Any design feature that was not an absolute necessity would have to go. The calculus of weight versus lifting power of the Saturn V was coldly tyrannical, and it went something like this: anything added to the LM, such as larger fuel tanks, made the craft heavier. That extra weight meant that more fuel was needed to propel it, and *that* required larger fuel tanks, and so forth. This was just one reason why the project soon felt like you were sharpening a pencil at both ends until nothing was left. The current design for the LM left it thousands of pounds overweight. Many of the more traditional solutions to these new problems would need to be turned inside out—and in the process, the thing would become *ugly.*

SOLUTIONS EMERGE

> **CHALLENGE:**
>
> Lighten the spacecraft—a lot.

One solution was to lose most of the windows. That amount of glass, a dozen or so square feet of thick, pressure-resistant quartz glass, weighed *a lot.* They would eliminate all but two small triangular windows. But how, then, would the astronauts be able to see the moon as it rushed up to meet them? Somehow the pilot would have to get much closer to the tiny windows.

Two flashes of inspiration occurred simultaneously. First, get rid of the seats! In the one-sixth gravity of the moon, the crew members did not need to sit, and this would save hundreds of pounds. They could stand the entire way—the journey down to the moon and the flight back were relatively brief. The astronauts could stand close enough to the tiny windows to see everything that they needed to see.

The hull design changed too: wrapping the metal around the minimum space that the astronauts needed resulted not in a sphere, but in something far more bizarre. The LM looked more like a fungus than a spacecraft. It was all flat surfaces and asymmetry, the bane of the aeronautical engineer. This admittedly ugly machine was a shape that only a mother—or an aeronautical engineer—could love. But it would work, and that was what mattered.

SOLUTION:

Again, think past long-held assumptions and resist the familiar; keep only what is needed to complete the task.

The lower stage also needed to be trimmed. When the engineers thought about it, they realized that the descent stage didn't need to be round—when they simply wrapped the design around a framework strong enough to hold landing legs to the crew compartment, it became an octagon, and its size and weight were dramatically reduced. Also, they realized that they did not need five legs, yet three were too few to assure stability when landing on a rocky surface. So they settled on four instead. Problem solved . . . but not without a lot of sweat.

As they labored to resolve the basic design issues, there was one overruling law: keep the crew members alive and bring them home. The LM was a two-stage machine: it would land on the moon with one engine in one structure, and depart using an upper stage with another engine, but the ascent or upper-stage engine was by far the more critical. Obviously both engines had to work perfectly the first time. If there were problems starting the descent engine, the crew members would simply return to the capsule and abort the landing before they got into danger. But the ascent engine would not be used until they had finished their long stay on the lunar surface. If it didn't light when they pushed the button, the two astronauts would become an involuntary part of NASA's first Apollo lunar museum. And there was another layer of complication here: the two stages had to be able to communicate with each other via wires and cables, but they would also have to separate cleanly and instantaneously when it was time to leave. Failure to unplug from the lower stage would be another astronaut killer. These kinds of nightmarish problems attended every basic decision and amplified the stakes. On top of that, there was a more traditional managerial problem: the workforce. Every bit of this new flying machine had to be crafted and assembled perfectly. Even if the NASA inspectors didn't catch a problem (which was bad enough), the slightest mistake or error could cause a failure—and a loss of life.

As if to underscore this point, the astronauts slated for Apollo

CHALLENGE:

Workmanship issues and employee dedication.

flights were being sent by NASA to contractors all over the country. There were two reasons for this. First, it allowed NASA—and the astronauts themselves—to see what was going on, make suggestions, and voice concerns. Second, it put a human face on the program. The latter worked perfectly. The Grumman workers, who were already giving their all to the LM program, became consumed by the notion of keeping the astronauts—*their* astronauts—safe.

SOLUTION:

Put a human face on the program.

The first astronaut assigned to Grumman was Fred Haise, who would eventually use the knowledge gained by his deep involvement in the Lunar Module program to get his crippled spacecraft home when *Apollo 13* used the module as a lifeboat. His intimate understanding of the LM and its inner workings went a long way toward saving his crew. When he first arrived at the Grumman plant, Haise was on a walk-through of the LM assembly area when he pulled one of the Grumman executives aside to make a request. The man looked surprised, saying something to the effect of, "Mr. Haise, hundreds of people are working on the LM!" Haise was undeterred . . . and later that day, he placed himself at the head of a line that snaked through the plant and well outside the door and beyond. He wanted to shake the hand of *every single person* who was working on the Lunar Module, and he did. It was a brilliant way to get the builders of this complex, fragile machine onto his team. None of them ever forgot this simple gesture—they built a perfect flying machine for "Fred."

GRINDING ONWARD

By 1965, the basic design of the LM had been worked out, and the moments of innovative brilliance were coming more slowly—the remaining design issues were more incremental in nature, and that much harder to solve. But there were still many decisions and design compromises that had to be made. These included the propulsion system (it needed 100 percent reliability, or the guys weren't coming home), life support (if this failed, they would have to abandon the mission), electronic guidance (this in an era in which computers still filled entire rooms), and a myriad of other things.

With just over three years until the first projected landing, the program was perilously behind schedule. This was a trip into the unknown, and each solution had to be tested and refined. This took time, a commodity that was in critically short supply. NASA was working on a martyred president's schedule—"Before the end of this decade"—and dealing with an increasingly unsupportive Congress. The Apollo program was by now devouring nearly 5 percent of the federal budget, and there had been talk of trimming Grumman's LM spending by up to 40 percent, all this at a time when the company was experiencing vast cost overruns. Time and money overshadowed everything that it did.

The issue of weight simply would not go away. The Saturn V's lifting power was a fixed constant, but other parts of the system, such as the Apollo capsule, were gaining weight rapidly—it had to be made of sterner stuff than the LM, as it would have to survive the crushing, fiery return to Earth. So the LM was put on a crash diet.

CHALLENGE:

LM weight issues persist.

This sounds simple; in practice, it was not. The LM was already a lightweight. The metal in its hull—aluminum and titanium—was in places scarcely thicker than a Coke can. The metal panels that were originally intended to cover the sides of the landing stage frame were gone, replaced with fluttery sheets of Mylar. This space-age Saran Wrap had no structural strength at all; it merely protected the innards of the landing stage from heat and cold. The whole thing was so delicate, so flimsy, that when the astronauts came to visit their future ride, they began calling it "the Aluminum Balloon." This was not intended as a compliment. Indeed, if a technician so much as dropped a screwdriver inside the cabin during assembly, it was likely to punch a hole through the side.

Yet it still was not light enough.

Kelly decided that weight was the ultimate enemy of the program, so he placed a bounty on pounds, then ounces, then *grams*. He would pay the Grumman workers for every bit of weight they saved—and not just the engineers. If a janitor came up with a way to save a bit of weight someplace, he or she would benefit from the bounty program just like anyone else.

SOLUTION:

Good old-fashioned financial incentives—a bounty on weight.

As a result, every piece in the Lunar Module was scrutinized. The hull panels, the landing gear, the hatches, the antennae—*everything* came under a critical eye. Tiny parts were milled down in the shop until they broke under the stress of merely holding together, then the machinist would back off until it was *just strong enough*. It was exacting, exhausting work, but still they soldiered on. They even resorted to *chemical* milling, literally dissolving parts until they were just a bit thinner.

In hindsight, Kelly figured that hundreds of thousands of dollars were spent in weight bounties at $25,000 per pound (and these were mid-1960s dollars). Still, they just barely made it. It was the first time that such an intensive effort had been made with any flying machine, but in the end it worked: the LM was finally svelte enough to fly. By the time they were done, parts of the ship's hull were quite literally the thickness of three sheets of aluminum foil. In fact, as one of the engineers amazed his teammates by pointing out that when the LM was pressurized, parts of it—including the hatch—*bulged*. The astronauts in attendance coined another unflattering name for the ship: the tissue-paper spacecraft.

CHALLENGE:

Every part is mission-critical.

As the weight issues were being worked out, hundreds of other, less obvious problems were being solved through highly innovative thinking—and some brute-force methods. The issue of separating the wiring between the LM stages when it was time to leave the moon was a good example. There was a five-inch-thick bundle of wires and cables between the descent stage and the ascent stage. When it was time to leave the moon, assuming that the ascent engine lit, this bundle of wires needed to disconnect, and *right now*. Plugs would have been the traditional solution, but NASA's experience with plugs was that they were unreliable and therefore absolutely unacceptable for this mission-critical application. The solution dated back to before the French revolution: a guillotine. Two long, sharp blades were fastened on either side of the cables—it looked like a high-tech hedge trimmer. When the time came to release the ascent stage, explosive charges were fired that slammed the blades home and slashed through the cables, resulting in a clean and complete cut—an elegant and simple solution that worked every time.

SOLUTION:

Design with extreme redundancy and simplicity wherever possible.

Another example of the nightmarish problems were the fuels. Propellants for the main engine and the maneuvering thrusters were toxic and corrosive. Even a slight residue of detergent used to clean the fuel tanks could cause them to explode when they were filled.

And the maneuvering thruster fuel lines—long and thin—leaked constantly. It was a constant battle, and in the end metal patches were applied right on the launchpad.

TRIUMPH

In 1968, the LM was scheduled for its first manned test, *Apollo 8*, but it was still too leaky and heavy, so that mission flew without it. But by early 1969, the Lunar Modules were finally ready to fly. *Apollo 9* tested one in Earth orbit, and *Apollo 10* performed a similar test in orbit around the moon. Then in July of 1969, *Apollo 11*'s LM, *Eagle*, landed on the moon. The machine performed perfectly, as it did in all subsequent flights up through *Apollo 17*, its final voyage. In fact along with the Saturn V booster, it was the only part of the Apollo system that never had a meaningful failure of any kind.

As a coda, there was the troubled journey of *Apollo 13*. Shortly after heading off to the moon, an oxygen tank on the Command Module exploded, crippling the spacecraft. Had it not been for the Lunar Module, with its extraordinary reliability and overengineered safety margins, the crew of three would never have survived the journey home. It was truly a lifeboat in space.

To Tom Kelly, that was reward enough.

INNOVATIONS

- Designed and built the first true spacecraft, intended to fly only in the vacuum of space and land on and return from the moon.
- Created change within the Grumman culture from design once/build many to an extremely specialized short-run project.

- Trained engineers to think in terms of lightweight nonaerodynamic spaceships instead of more familiar streamlined warplanes.
- Implemented a program of radical weight reduction for the LM and utilized advanced technologies to accomplish this.
- Designed redundant systems for mission-critical applications, with a success rate of 100 percent.
- Where redundancy was not possible, overengineered systems to high levels of reliability, while maintaining weight limits.

CHAPTER 8

TAMING THE DRAGON: THE F-1 ROCKET ENGINE

CHALLENGES

- Design the largest rocket engine in history and build it.
- Test the engine without causing it to explode every time.
- Solve tremendous instability problems without much data.
- Find a way to cool and lubricate the engine with nonstandard means.
- Stay on schedule while working with completely unknown quantities.

DARING THE HEAVENS

It seemed that everything about going to the moon was bigger, flashier, and newer than ever before, and certainly more dangerous. The plans for Apollo were audacious, almost as if we were daring the heavens to stop us. The astronauts were larger-than-life heroes, and NASA liked it that way. And the rocket—well, that was truly in a class of its own. With the destructive force of a small atom bomb if it exploded, and both larger and heavier than a navy destroyer—that flew—the Saturn V dwarfed everything that had gone before.

To power that rocket, NASA needed huge rocket engines. Fortunately, a few years before Kennedy announced the plan to win the moon, the U.S. Air Force had been feeling a bit of "booster envy" vis-à-vis the Soviet Union and decided that it might need something a bit larger than it had in the stockpile. And it had to be way bigger than the already large rockets that the Russians were flying.

CHALLENGE:

How to surpass Soviet superiority in rocket power in record time.

The Air Force selected Rocketdyne in California to build a new power plant for America's ICBMs, a monster that would create a million pounds of thrust and embarrass even Soviet efforts. Rocketdyne was a unit of North American Aviation, which would soon be building the Apollo spacecraft and the second stage of the booster. The company knew what it was doing. But this new assignment was well beyond anything that *anyone* had done before.

This new rocket engine was bigger, hotter, thirstier, and vastly more powerful than anything that had previously been attempted. Called simply the F-1, its sheer enormity was hard to grasp. In an era when a standing person could look down at most rocket engines, a whole committee of engineers could hold a meeting inside the exhaust nozzle of the F-1. It was that grand.

The design started out as most did: as an evolution of the same engine that had powered von Braun's V2 rocket during World War II. Rocketdyne would simply scale everything up—as it had been doing for more than a decade now—and the power would increase with the size. Of course, the engineers knew that it would not be that easy (nothing in spaceflight ever was), but even they did not have any idea just how challenging it would become. It would take every bit of innovative thinking that the best minds in the free world could muster to tame the beast once things got rolling.

SOLUTION:

Think big—choose to increase power by almost a factor of *10* for a healthy reserve. Scale up existing designs where possible.

Early on, the test engine, dubbed "King Kong," could run for only a few seconds before the 5,000-degree flame would burn through the thick metal housing. But these early tests told the engineers a few things. First, a different design would be needed for the rocket nozzle and other parts to keep them from melting—the solid metal parts from World War II designs would not work. Second, scaling up the overall design of the engine meant scaling up the challenges as well. It was not as simple as making everything larger.

The engineers tried new designs and stepped up the testing. This was the era of massive and slow computers, and even with the help of these machines, rocket engine design was as much an art as a science. You built them, tested them, and, when they blew up, collected the fragments and tried to figure out what had gone wrong. In fact, the very day that Kennedy made his most famous moon speech, one of Rocketdyne's engines blew itself to pieces. It was a rough-and-ready approach to power-plant design.

CHALLENGE:

How to test something that is basically a controlled bomb of enormous proportions.

Here was the challenge now that America had decided to go to the moon: to design and build the largest rocket engine in the world, capable of 1.5 million pounds of thrust (the next largest U.S. rocket engine of this type created about 200,000 pounds), or the equivalent of 32 million horsepower. It would have to run for at least 10 minutes without exploding (although in flight it never ran for more than 2.5 minutes, the designers wanted a solid safety margin). It must be safe enough to bet the lives of America's hottest heroes on and 100 percent reliable. It was no small order.

The list of innovations involved in creating the F-1, which became

SOLUTION:

(1) Test everything until it fails, and learn from this. Then, (2) invent new ways to predict imminent failure to avoid destroying the machine you are testing.

one of the most reliable rocket engines in the world, is long and filled with incredible minutiae. But the major ideas and brainstorms that changed the course of America's space program are what Robert Biggs remembers best from his decade on the F-1 project.

FACING THE MONSTER

When Biggs arrived at Rocketdyne in the late 1950s, he was still a young man. Having spent his time in the military, he skipped finishing college to get a job, ending up at Rocketdyne, where he was put to work on various defense projects before moving to the F-1. At the time, he had no idea that this new, enormous engine would go to the moon, or that he would spend the next 55 years of his life building rocket engines (he moved to the shuttle main engine program after nine years on Apollo). He loved each and every program.

The F-1 was a heady assignment. At that point in time, the United States was still trying to orbit the grapefruit-sized *Vanguard*, which was powered by a rocket engine with 30,000 pounds of thrust, or about one-fiftieth the power of the engine he was setting out to build. In 1957, a 10 percent increase in thrust was a big deal. And he certainly hoped that the F-1 would be more reliable—of eleven Vanguard launch attempts, only three were ultimately successful.

The basic components of rocket engines were well established. Such an engine needed fuel (in this case, kerosene and liquid oxygen), pumps, a combustion chamber, and a nozzle. But as the size grew, so did the complexity, which required more pumps, valves, solenoids, hydraulic and lubricating systems, sensors, and much more. The result was a complex beast of a machine.

Biggs's first assignment was the engine's start-up sequence. The time it took the fuels to ignite once they were inside the giant motor resulted in acoustic shock waves that shook it to bits—it was that big. The normal way to start the burn was a spark plug, but he needed something more dramatic. He invented a small bomb that lit the fuel mist inside the the combustion chamber all at once—and it worked. Beautifully.

CHALLENGE:

Engines are continuing to fail in tests because of explosions—clearly someone has missed something important. How do you prevent this?

As Biggs and his team were working on these procedures, he noticed a problem. At first he thought that surely someone else would have noticed something so obvious if it were truly an issue, but apparently nobody had. There had been a series of failures of the liquid oxygen (lox) turbopump. Three of them had exploded on the test stand. After looking at the data from a series of engine test starts, Biggs noticed that when the pump started up and began moving the huge volumes of lox that the massive engine ingested, there was a dangerous pressure spike. The valves needed to be opened sooner. This was a matter of milliseconds, and it had to be done with precision. But now he saw another problem: when all that fluid came galloping into the huge pipes that fed the monster engine, the raw force of the liquids would cause the lines to rupture, and ruptured fuel lines on rockets mean fires, and ultimately large explosions.

Sometimes innovation is proactive, and sometimes it's reactive. Sometimes it's complex; at other times, it's simple. Biggs thought it over and decided to cause a "leak"—he would open the valve early, just a crack, to let some lox flow into the pipe before allowing the pump to move the gross bulk of it through. The result? Less empty space for the lox to come crashing into, and no more ruptures. Big issues can have small resolutions.

SOLUTION:

Look where others may not have. Then look again where others have, at data that may hold secrets to improving results. Then adapt designs and procedures to produce a safer, more successful alternative.

MULTIPLE PROBLEMS, ONE SOLUTION

Another goal, and an overriding one, was simplification. On an engine of this size, design decisions that worked on smaller rocket engines resulted in a weight penalty that was prohibitive when they were scaled up. An example was lubrication systems. Normally, an oil tank with a pump would keep the moving parts in a rocket engine slippery, and that's critically important. The main fuel turbine for the F-1 engine was a 55,000-horsepower monster, spinning just shy of 6,000 rpm, with the largest turbine blades ever used in flight. The fuels coming through the pump were chilled to many hundreds of degrees below zero, but the turbine itself could get up into the hundreds of degrees Fahrenheit. Traditional lubricants would freeze or boil off, and the result would be catastrophic. Any solution the engineers thought of was complex and heavy. They needed a breakthrough.

CHALLENGE:

Build an enormously complex piece of engineering while observing weight limits and restraining tendencies toward increasing complexity.

Then they had an inspiration. They needed *something*—oil, grease, or beer, for that matter—between the bearing faces. It did not have to be a traditional petroleum-based product. So they settled on using the rocket's *own fuel* to lubricate the bearings. This is not as crazy as it sounds, for as important as it was to create a film separating adjacent parts, carrying *heat* away from those parts was just as urgent. And, in a delightful case of serendipity, the fuel needed to be preheated anyway. Two birds, one stone. This would become a familiar, and ingenious, refrain in the F-1 program. Soon, instead of blowing test rigs to bits, the turbine was humming along, transporting 25,000 gallons of liquid oxygen and 15,000 gallons of kerosene each minute.

SOLUTION:

Find ways for single elements of the system to perform multiple tasks, even if it involves unorthodox approaches.

But the clever engineers had still other tasks for the 6,000 gallons of fluids that the engine would consume very second. One job was to keep the enormous rocket nozzle of the engine from destroying itself.

While the combustion chamber had to withstand terrible temperatures and pressures, another problem area was where the exhaust exited into the thin-walled rocket nozzle. Temperatures and pressures were off the charts. The rocket nozzle channeled the gases from the combustion chamber in an ever-expanding plume to maximize thrust. When they did so, the walls of the nozzle could melt, and quickly. One of the big problems von Braun had faced in the V2 days was burn-through of the nozzles. The advance that would solve this problem had actually been worked out on earlier engine designs, but as with so many parts of this program, never at a scale even approaching that needed for the F-1. It was called regenerative cooling.

CHALLENGE:

How to cool critical parts of a red-hot rocket engine without adding more weight or complexity.

When this solution is explained to most people, they're surprised. In short, the engineers would run explosive fuel through a hollow rocket nozzle to cool it. The top half of the nozzle was made of hundreds and hundreds of hollow tubes running from the combustion chamber down to the midsection of the cone. These tubes were about an inch in diameter and joined at the bottom. When the engine fired, cold fuel was pumped through the pipes. In effect, the entire rocket nozzle—the second most violent place on a rocket engine—was a two-layer foil-thin cone filled with explosive rocket fuel. It sounds crazy, but if you kept the cold fuel flowing, it carried away much of the heat that was generated when it was ejected, now hellishly hot, from the combustion chamber just a few feet away.

This process also served to preheat the fuel to a temperature that was more amenable to combustion. Once again, the engineers were solving multiple problems with a single, elegant solution.

There were still two more innovative economies in the use of rocket fuel. Remember the small amounts used to fire up the turbine? The initial thought was to simply dump the exhaust by-products off to the side. But then the engineers thought, "Hey, there has to be a better way to get rid of that stuff." And, as it turned out, they had a concurrent problem: the bottom half of the rocket nozzle, which was just sheet metal, not fuel-filled tubes, needed to be cooled as well. It didn't need nearly as much cooling as the top half, as the exhaust plume cooled rapidly as it expanded. But it did need to be cooled, and the use of tubes of liquid fuel to cool this area carried an unacceptable weight penalty. The engineers thought it over, and realized that by the time the turbine exhaust traveled through a pipe from the top (gas turbine) to the bottom (lower nozzle) of the engine, it was substantially cooler than the nightmare of fire coming out of the combustion chamber. Why not use it to cool the lower part of the nozzle? So they tried it. Large ducts from the turbine exhaust ports to the middle of the huge nozzle were added, looking like a giant metal octopus wrapping its arms around its middle. The cooler turbine exhaust formed a gaseous blanket inside the lower half of the nozzle, protecting it from the heat of the main exhaust. It was another seemingly crazy idea that worked brilliantly, and it was an economical use of what would otherwise have been a waste product.

SOLUTION:

Use *everything*—multiple times if possible. Recognizing that temperature is relative, channel warm waste gases to hotter areas that you are trying to protect, where they can be used productively before being released.

The final nontraditional use of rocket fuel came up when von Braun specified that the four outboard engines on the Saturn V first stage needed to be steerable. In the past, steering rockets with aerodynamic fins had been tried, with mixed results. But with the kind of power and speed inherent in the giant Saturn V, fins would not be sufficiently effective. Gimbaled engines—that could swing one way or another to steer the rocket—had been used on other boosters, but the F-1 was so large that traditional methods of steering the giant engines were too heavy. So the engineers got to thinking.

You have probably already guessed the answer. In another rerouting of the highly explosive fuel, they dared to use it as hydraulic fluid. Kerosene was pumped and valved into huge pistons to steer the giant rocket—they literally swung the entire engine assemblies to and fro using pressurized rocket fuel, which was then routed to the combustion chamber for fiery disposal. Truly ingenious.

CHALLENGE:

Solve apparently impossible engineering problems that were at the root of the project.

As these mechanical design details were being worked out, Biggs and his team were still testing the engines and having terrible problems. The largest potential showstopper for the F-1 was a nasty bit of business called *combustion instability*. The issue was this: all rocket engines tend to burn fuel a bit unevenly; with thousands of gallons of fuel pouring through, mixing, and then burning in less time than it takes you to say "ignition," some pockets burned hotter and faster than others. This created not only hot spots (which were in themselves dangerous), but also sonic waves. These waves propagated across the large combustion chamber, further disrupting the even burning of the fuel and rattling the hell out of the engine. And, as with so many things involving the F-1, what was an annoyance with smaller engines was a rocket destroyer with the F-1. The instability got so bad and engines were blowing up so frequently that they had to install vibration sensors to shut the test engines down before they shook themselves into a cataclysmic explosion.

The goal of the engineers was to damp out these irregularities within 400 milliseconds. But in 1959, they would have been happy just to be able to keep the engines from shutting down or exploding in tests.

A variety of factors were causing this, and once again, they were all things that became greatly and dangerously magnified when the engine design was made larger. One was the injector plate, a flat metal disk three feet wide and four inches thick that lived inside the combustion chamber. It looked like a giant manhole cover with 6,300 holes drilled through it. When the two fuels—the supercold liquid oxygen and the ambient-temperature kerosene—entered the combustion chamber, they could not simply be dumped there. They needed to be pumped through this injector plate, which then forced the fluids into little fans to assure even and effective combustion. The engineers tried changing the angle of the fans; they tried changing the size of the orifices. They tried adding metal baffles that ran from the center of the plate to the edges. For two years they tried hundreds of designs. At one point, a NASA inspector is said to have come upon a group of metalworkers—some of whom were reportedly high school dropouts—tooling one of the baffle plates. When he asked them what they were doing, they said that the engineers had walked away in disgust and said, "Try whatever you want." It was that bad.

And all along, the testing continued. Sometimes they would do two or three tests a day. Amidst the failures, some tests ended well, with an incremental improvement being made and a small structural change proved. But overall, it was test, try something else, test, and test again. It was driving Biggs and his team crazy.

Eventually they began to realize that this combustion instability issue was so hit-and-miss that they might still be testing in 1999 and still not have it figured out—it was a seemingly chance occurrence, but a potentially disastrous one. How could you test new designs for something that happened at random, even though all other factors were equal?

SOLUTION:

Be creative—if you can learn how to reliably cause a seemingly random problem, you can probably learn to solve it.

And then the engineers got a wonderful, bizarre, and slightly malevolent idea: bombs.

A BOLD ANSWER TO A FINAL PROBLEM

If one wanted to set up acoustic disturbances in the enormous combustion chamber, what better way was there than to set off an explosion of a known amount in a consistent location within the maelstrom of fire that was at the F-1's core? It seemed easy enough, if slightly twisted.

They tried various loads in dozens of ways. Eventually they settled on a three-inch steel tube filled with high explosive. But how to insert it into the engine without its going off too soon?

They tried everything they could think of, including putting it on the end of a pipe and jamming it up the throat of the combustion chamber. In the end, they found a place to mount the charge within the combustion chamber that was at a relatively low temperature during the first few moments of ignition, and from which they were able to run detonation leads.

When they started the next test, the concrete test stand shook as the thousands of gallons of fuel began to flow. Then there was a cough and roar as the fuels ignited and a burst of yellow-orange flame enveloped the bottom of the test stand. As the thrust built and the ground shook, the engineers watched the readouts nervously—at this point in the game, nobody knew quite what to expect. Then, when the pressure in the combustion chamber reached a stable level of about 1,100 pounds per square inch, the bomb would be ignited, causing the chamber pressure to spike to more than 4,000 psi. Part of the issue with combustion instability, besides the thrust pulsing and vibration, was this sudden and nasty increase in chamber pressure. So this artificially induced acoustic wave replicated that condition perfectly and somewhat predictably.

Then they would wait and watch. It was just a matter of seconds—in fact, milliseconds. From the beginnings of this issue in the late 1950s to 1961, hundreds of tests were conducted; the goal was to damp out the instabilities within 400 milliseconds. By the time it was over, they had it down to one-quarter of that, or 100 ms. It was a case of total mastery of a technical problem, with bizarre, yet truly innovative solutions.

By the end of 1968, they had tested the F-1 thousands of times. It had flown on the Saturn V rocket twice—two tests, both with minor issues. A phenomenon similar to (but different from) the combustion instability (it was called "pogo") had crept in. The rocket's thrust would pulse, shaking the whole Saturn V violently. It turned out that the pogo effect was the result of resonance within the actual structure of the Saturn's first stage. While it was never entirely eliminated, it was tuned down to acceptable limits—a large, structural version of tuning guitar strings. The shaking did not stop, but it decreased enough. Again, good was good enough.

When pressed by nervous NASA management, von Braun was sanguine—he felt that they had licked the issues sufficiently and that the rocket was ready to fly with men aboard. And just in time, too—for the end of 1968 was looming, the lunar module was still too heavy and problem-plagued to fly, and the CIA had just released a classified report that indicated that the Soviets might be nearly ready to send a crew on a trajectory to loop the moon. And although there would be no Russian landing, it would steal much of Apollo's thunder.

So after just two partially successful launch tests, and with just a few months of preparation, three astronauts boarded von Braun's giant rocket, complete with its complement of five adolescent F-1 engines, and blasted off toward the moon. They would ultimately go into orbit around that body, and famously read from Genesis on Christmas Eve. It was the flight of *Apollo 8*, and the F-1s behaved perfectly. In fact, with the exception of a bit of irritating pogo-bouncing on a couple of later flights, the F-1 ultimately had a perfect record of safety and performance.

As a postscript, and a bit of inverse innovation (if there is such a thing), a group of NASA technicians recently entered the Smithsonian's National Air and Space Museum and wandered over to the F-1 engine on display. Their tools and winches made quite a show. Within a few days, they had dismounted and removed the gas generator that drove the giant turbine from the top of the old rocket engine exhibit, and weeks later they were firing up freshly made copies of that 50-year-old design at a test facility. As with so much of the Apollo program, records of fabrication and testing are not as complete as the engineers might like, and the best way to avoid reinventing the wheel—in this case, building yet another huge rocket engine for the twenty-first century—was to take an engine from 1965 off the shelf and remind themselves how it worked. It was a fitting epitaph for the efforts of so many dedicated and clever people decades before . . . and at that moment, Robert Biggs was a very proud man.

INNOVATIONS

- Recognized that more powerful rockets do not result from simply "scaling up" existing ones.
- Designed new ways of moving and burning unprecedented amounts of rocket fuel.
- Learned ways to test engines without destroying them.
- Found the "sweet spot" between purely quantifiable design and engineering techniques and inspiration/intuition.
- Innovated new techniques in metallurgy, machining, casting, and fabricating items for use in high-temperature and high-pressure environments beyond anything that had previously been attempted at this scale.
- Invented new techniques in cooling, hydraulic steering, and lubrication, using the very fuel that the engines would later burn to accomplish these tasks.
- Found new and innovative ways to manage a project that dealt with vast unknowns, while still keeping the company solvent and costs (relatively) under control.

CHAPTER 9

THE BIG SQUEEZE: THE SATURN V'S INCREDIBLE SECOND STAGE

CHALLENGES

- Fulfill two large contracts for NASA at a time when one was more than most companies could handle.
- Design and build, on time and on budget, a highly advanced rocket stage with preset—and unrealistic—design parameters.
- Adapt to changes in weight and performance specifications when changes come weekly, without incurring cost overruns or delays.
- Invent new technologies to accomplish all of these requirements without compromising safety or performance, or raising cost.
- Above all, make sure that these new and untried technologies are safe and reliable.

A DARING GAMBLE

North American Aviation (NAA) had always been out on the cutting edge of flight and aircraft design. The company made its mark in World War II, taking the slow, underperforming P-40 fighter (the only modern fighter in America's arsenal in 1941) and transforming it into the world-beating P-51 that played a pivotal role in bringing both Germany and Japan to their knees. Since then, North American Aviation, or NAA, had continued to blaze new trails in aircraft design, dashing ahead where more staid companies only crept. NAA built the hot rods of the skies, and the ultimate exemplar of this was the X-15 rocket plane. Flying higher and faster than anything that had gone before, the craft flew high enough to earn its pilots astronaut wings. There was even talk of equipping the rocket plane for orbital spaceflight. Of course, that was before NASA threw in its lot with the Mercury program and its stubby little capsule. And one man had been primarily responsible for NAA's involvement with NASA: Harrison Storms.

Storms was a driven man. He was smart enough to do just about anything he set his mind to, and from an early age, his father had let it be known that he intended his son to become an engineer. He accomplished this with distinction, graduating with undergraduate and graduate degrees in mechanical engineering from Northwestern. Soon thereafter, he rounded out his résumé with another degree, a master's of aeronautical engineering from Caltech. By 1941, he was working for North American, and by 1958, the year of NASA's formation, he was the vice president and chief engineer of NAA's Los Angeles operations.

Storms went to the mat to win the contract for the X-15 despite the reservations of his corporate masters. North American's bosses built airplanes that could be mass-produced on assembly lines for great profits, not one-off spacecraft. But the X-15 contract had set the stage for far greater things to come, reminding the NASA brass of how effective NAA had been in turning the tide of aerial combat during the war. With the Apollo program cranking up, despite a highly competitive bidding process, North American seemed to do *extraordinarily* well in winning contracts once things got going.

Some people thought *too* well—Storms's methods were somewhat suspect in certain circles.

In the end, the company won two major contracts for Apollo. The flashiest one was for the Command and Service Module. This was the Apollo capsule and its support and propulsion unit. And talk about sexy—not only did it look like something out of an updated Buck Rogers film, but it carried the astronauts and was, after all, at the pointy end of the rocket.

The other contract, however, proved in many ways to be even more challenging and required vast amounts of innovation where one might least expect it. This was the contract for the Saturn V rocket's second stage, called the S-II (that is, S-2). It sat atop the monster first stage, which was being built by Boeing and von Braun's Germans at Huntsville, with its five massive F-1 engines. And it sat below the S-IVB stage (which, despite the label, was the third stage), which in turn carried the Command Module and the Lunar Module. The S-II was, quite literally, squeezed between the other two. And this simple fact would almost kill the entire effort, and, by extension, many of the people involved in its creation.

CHALLENGE:

Design and construct a rocket stage at the cutting edge of mechanical and materials engineering.

One could be excused for not being overly impressed by the S-II stage at first. A quick look reveals a mere interim rocket stage that looks like an oversized fireplug with five medium-sized rocket engines on the business end. It's just a cylinder with nozzles. If the massive first stage was the muscle-bound hero of the beach, the S-II was his trusty—and rarely flirted with—sidekick. But to leave it at that is to vastly shortchange the miracle of engineering innovation within.

It cannot be overstressed that this was innovation under fire. The S-II stage, as the last major contract awarded for the Apollo system, was the one place where the shortcomings of the items above and below it—the rest of the rocket—had to be accommodated. The S-II stage also rapidly became a "pacing item," that is, an anchor dragging behind Apollo. If anything other than the Lunar Module was likely to push the first moon landing into 1970—that is, into the "wrong decade"—it was the S-II. The pressure was overwhelming, to put it mildly.

SOLUTION:

Discard assumptions about traditional rocket stage design; rethink everything.

But to Storms, it was a study in the application of force—force as in brute force engineering . . . force as in the massive power of hydrogen burning with oxygen . . . and force as in the application of his own intense personality.

The dimensions of the S-II had been outlined by NASA prior to the award of the contract. This was less profound than met the eye, however, and the diameter of the stage kept increasing to accommodate the ever-increasing weight of the parts of the craft above: the S-IVB stage, the Lunar Module, and NAA's own Command and Service Module.

Additionally, other than specifying two tanks of bitterly cold fuel and five rocket engines below (these to be supplied by an NAA subsidiary, Rocketdyne), how to pull off the engineering was an open question.

When Storms looked at the project before his full-court press to win the bid, it was overwhelming. Here was a machine the size of a grain silo—and not just a tank with nozzles, but a complex, intricate machine with hundreds of thousands of parts that would need to be built to Swiss-watch specifications. And it had to be light enough and strong enough to fly into space. Atop it would ride almost 350,000 pounds of moon-landing spacecraft; below it would be 7.5 million pounds of rocket thrust—pounding, brutal acceleration—that could twist the entire stage to scrap metal in an instant.

Moderating any design approach was the knowledge that any changes in the weight (especially above) or the size of the rest of the rocket could cause a major redesign at any time. And if NASA proceeded true to form, changes in the rest of the rocket would be nearly continuous. Clearly, new and breakthrough thinking would be required.

INNOVATION IN DESPERATION

Basic liquid-fueled rocket design had been evolving since the 1930s and accelerated dramatically in the 1950s. But for something the size and scope of the S-II stage, there was little experience to draw upon. As with so much of Apollo, this would be designed from whole cloth.

Storms looked at the parts of the rocket that his stage would be sandwiched in between. Below the S-II was von Braun's S-IC stage. It was of truly mythic proportions, in keeping with the Apollo moniker. Standing 138 feet high and ultimately 33 feet in diameter, this monster would be powered by five of the mightiest rocket engines ever built. It consumed kerosene at the rate of 15 tons per second and produced 7.5 million pounds of thrust. But for all that, it was generally a scaled-up, traditional design, with a direct lineage from World War II's V2 rocket. Sure, it had been refined and enlarged to gargantuan proportions, but from a high-tech perspective, it was a huge version of what had gone before—a conservative design that was typical of von Braun's Huntsville empire.

For one thing, it used very conventional fuel—kerosene with liquid oxygen (lox) as an oxidizer, allowing it to burn in the thin upper atmosphere. The kerosene was roughly at room temperature, making it easy to store, with only the supercold lox needing special handling. The structure holding all this together was ingenious, but not lightly built or particularly elegant from an engineering standpoint. The German designers, who were working hand in hand with the prime contractor, Boeing, tended to overengineer their rockets with wide margins for safety. This was great from the perspective of the guys riding the rocket, but for the people stuck with designing the rest of it, the weight penalty exacted by this type of design was punishing.

Above the S-II stage was the S-IVB stage. This was powered by a single smaller engine, the same power plant that the S-II would use, but the S-II would utilize five of them. This engine was remarkable mostly because of the power it produced for its size, as a result of the high-energy fuels it employed. Unlike the first stage, the S-II and S-IVB stages would use liquid hydrogen and liquid oxygen for fuel. These had the distinct advantage of containing twice the energy of kerosene and lox. However, both liquid hydrogen and lox were cryogenic, meaning that they had to be stored onboard as supercold liquids. To accomplish this, they would have to be maintained at temperatures of hundreds of degrees below zero—about minus 300 degrees Fahrenheit for the lox and minus 425 degrees Fahrenheit for the hydrogen. This was a challenge, especially when designers were being vigilant about weight. And the two fuels hated each other, as the 125-degree temperature differential caused the colder fuel to boil off or the warmer one to freeze, both of which were unacceptable and could lead to disaster.

CHALLENGE:

While observing rigid specifications, build a machine of unprecedented power and lightness.

The S-IVB stage would provide the final boost that Apollo needed to leave Earth and head off to the moon. Its main challenge was that it needed to be restartable, and it would fire at least twice before being cast adrift. These innovations added weight. By the time NAA was sitting down to *bid* the S-II, the upper-stage design was already headed into production. And while it was ingenious in its own right, it was also heavy. Again, the S-II—late to the party—would have to absorb the weight penalty.

Finally, there were the Lunar Module (LM) and the Command/Service Module (CSM). Grumman was having its own drama with the design and construction of the LM out in Bethpage, New York, but the important fact was that, like most of Apollo, the LM was gaining weight at a steady pace.

Ironically, the CSM was being designed and built by North American just across town from where the S-II would ultimately be constructed. The CSM was also gaining pounds despite all NAA's efforts at streamlining the machine. So in a very real way, NAA had become its own enemy.

THE BREAKTHROUGH

Traditional rocket design, most of which was derived from von Braun's V2s in post–World War II analysis and development, used two huge tanks to hold the fuels. In the massive S-IC stage, two egg-shaped tanks—33-foot cylinders with rounded, dome-shaped end caps—were stacked to hold the fuels. While these were immense, they were basically refinements of what had gone before—and, as noted, heavy as hell. Storms knew that he would need to innovate, at least in an evolutionary way.

He pondered the question of how to lighten and shorten the S-II. The benefits of lightness are obvious; shortening it would also save weight, but, perhaps more important, would serve to strengthen the stage, as it would have less tendency to torque and flex, and possibly break up under stress. But if he used the traditional, tried-and-proven twin tank design being employed in the first stage, it would add 10 extra feet in length and more than 4,000 pounds to the S-II. He needed something different.

SOLUTION:

Improve on an existing idea: utilize a single bulkhead as others had done, but at a scale almost twice as large. Invent new techniques to construct it.

The inspiration actually came from the S-IVB design, then being executed over at Douglas Aircraft, also in Los Angeles. It too used hydrogen and lox as propellant, but unlike the twin-tank design of the first stage, the two fuels were separated by just one wall, or bulkhead. This saved a lot of weight and shortened the stage as desired. But the S-IVB stage was only 22 feet in diameter and had the luxury of using fairly traditional materials and fabrication for the structure, including the common bulkhead. Storms was skating out onto thin ice in considering this design for the huge S-II.

In the end, he found himself describing his design to a roomful of reluctant, terrified-looking engineers. The S-II would use the common bulkhead design on a scale that had never been tried before. To achieve the necessary strength within the allowable weight—and these allowances were almost impossibly low—he would use two very thin sheets of aluminum alloy with a plastic honeycomb between them. North American had pioneered the use of honeycomb structures on the B-70 Mach 3 bomber project years before, but not with plastic and never within these hostile environments. But there it was; the idea landed on the table between ranks of doubting minds. They didn't much like it, but they agreed that there was just no other way.

CHALLENGE:

Incorporate new designs, materials, and fabrication methods to make the stage more efficient than anything before.

Next up was the design of the hull. Traditional aeronautical techniques, such as flush riveting and traditional welding of sheet metal that contained the fuel tanks, were too heavy. The design of this unit would have to be a decade ahead of its time, and virtually every part of the S-II and the machines and techniques needed to create it required innovative thinking and solutions. The hull—which would also serve as the fuel tank walls—would need to be very strong and light. But Storms had an idea about that, too.

The tried-and-true methodology was to use traditional aircraft-grade aluminum alloy with separate tanks inside. To prevent the cryogenic fuels from boiling out, and to keep the aluminum skin from becoming brittle because of the cold, you insulated the structure from the cold chemicals inside.

But Storms and his team decided to use a newer aluminum alloy, 2014-T6, that was strong enough and light enough to use, not just as the skin of the rocket stage, but also as the tank walls. He could then insulate the stage from the *outside* instead of the inside, and the whole shebang would be a model of design efficiency. It was a great idea . . . but, like so much in the Apollo program, it was harder to implement than to conceive.

SOLUTION:

Seek simple and evolutionary solutions to multiple problems. Use a metal alloy that, when filled with freezing rocket fuel, becomes stronger but not brittle, and can act not just as a fuselage but as the fuel tank wall as well—a double win.

Nonetheless, it was sound thinking, and his team would earn a huge distinction besides the right to build the S-II: the Saturn V's second stage was on its way to officially becoming the most efficient design for a flying machine, in terms of weight versus strength, of all time.

BUILDING IT—STANDING UP

While Storms had been clever in wrestling the S-II and the Command and Service Module contracts from NASA, he now needed to build them. At the time, these, along with the Lunar Module, were the most complex machines on the planet. One, the CSM, would be a masterpiece of miniaturization and complexity, a phone-booth-sized capsule that would safely transport three men from the Earth to the moon and back, including the fiery, 5,000°F reentry. The Apollo capsule alone had more than two million parts, including life support, the first portable digital computer, cameras, fuel supplies, and so forth. It was, like the LM, something from the next century.

Building these machines was an endeavor like none other that had been undertaken by NAA up until now. It would later build the space shuttle and other high-tech one-offs, but at this point in time, it had been used to making a living designing and fabricating airplanes that were produced on an assembly line—lots of them. Now the company had the task of building a handful of machines that would take many times the R&D of the P-51 fighter. NAA needed brainpower—and lots of it.

CHALLENGE:

Transform an assembly-line operation into a high-tech prototyping organization, in which everything will be new and more complex than ever before.

So Storms did what he knew would serve him and NAA the best—he made like a pirate and raided first the other divisions of North American, then other aerospace companies, for the best and brightest people he could find. Cost was not yet an issue; he had to have the best. It got to the point where the heads of the other divisions, and even the other aerospace contractors, were calling his boss asking for him to be collared. But he soon had built a team of uncanny intelligence. And even with this, the completion of these two contracts was a very close thing. By the time they hit full stride, his workforce would number well over 30,000, and the budgets for the two contracts would have quadrupled.

SOLUTION:

Seek the best and the brightest. If you cannot find them within your operation, look to other divisions within the company for high-performing people before seeking outsiders.

As the design for the S-II came together, it was clear that the thing would be far too flimsy to construct on its side, the way the other stages—and most rockets up to that time—were fabricated. The team needed to build it standing up or the hull components would deform under their own weight. This was a preview of the kinds of delicate, and at times desperate, challenges before them.

They set the alloy sheets vertically as planned, and began welding around their circumference. Then, at about the 80 percent mark, there was a pop and a groan as the metal deformed. The heat of welding had caused it to bend out of shape, and they had to start over. The problem recurred.

As with so much of Apollo, Storms resorted to a brute-force solution. The team built a jig to hold the hull in place, top and bottom, with *15,000* setscrews, spaced one inch apart, for the entire 100-foot circumference. The S-II was mounted on a turntable so that it could slowly turn past the welder to accomplish the half-mile of welds on the external hull. It did not deform; however, nothing is noted about the sanity of the technicians who had to adjust the 15,000 setscrews.

KEEPING YOUR COOL

Now that the main structure had been built, it needed to be insulated from outside temperatures. But when the insulation was applied to the outer skin and the tank was filled with cryogenic fuels, the hull became so cold that little air bubbles that existed between the insulation and the metal itself *liquefied*—the fuel-chilled hull literally turned any outside air that was trapped nearby into a fluid. This caused the insulation to peel off in sheets, and this was a game-stopper for a flying machine.

The team developed an insulation that could be sprayed directly onto the hull, rather than applied in sheets as had been planned. This meant, however, that it had to be scraped and ground down to the proper shape and thickness once it cured—not an easy task on a 33-foot-wide cylinder. The task became as much a sculptor's art as an engineer's one.

Once the outer hull was ready, the intertank bulkhead could be installed. Recall that this was a single-wall sandwich structure that would serve as the top of the lox tank and the bottom of the liquid hydrogen tank all-in-one. Simple, right? Not on your life.

The basic structure as envisioned by Storms's team was made up of two thin aluminum domes separated by a layer of phenolic, or plastic-impregnated cloth. The phenolic would be a honeycomb design, and very resistant to deforming under the temperature extremes as well as an excellent insulator between the warring fuel temperatures.

But nobody had ever thought of trying to create lightweight, flight-rated aluminum domes of this size before. By now, the final specifications of the S-II stage were set—it needed to be 33 feet in diameter to match the first stage. This was the end of a series of changes in size that had driven them nuts. At least it was finally set in stone, but it was a huge chasm to fill.

CHALLENGE:

How to form huge, wafer-thin metal sheets into a compound curve.

The bulkhead domes were to be constructed of 12 pie slices, or gores, of aluminum alloy. These would be incredibly thin—about 1/4 inch at the rim and less than 1/32 inch at the point. The shape was a compound curve, almost a cup shape, like a giant inverted leaf that got thinner at the tip. And it had to be perfect. Nobody even had a machine that could *make a machine* to manufacture the part. So they set their minds to the task, and in one meeting someone mentioned, possibly only half-seriously, using explosives to form the things. The suggestion, on the face of it, sounded crazy . . . and therefore just might work.

Within a week, they had found a huge 60,000-gallon water tank down at El Toro Marine Air Station, not far from where they were building the S-II. They made a master form of the gore and sank it to the bottom of the tank. When the flimsy alloy sheets for the gores arrived, they lowered one of them into the tank and positioned it over the form. It hovered there, wiggling a bit in the currents of cold water because of its extreme thinness.

Primacord—basically an explosive rope—was positioned above the sheet metal. This was normally used by the military to cut through trees and blow through walls; with the explosive force dispersed by the water, it was the perfect choice. There was a short countdown, and then *wham*, 60,000 gallons of water thudded to the sides of the tank and a geyser leaped from the top. They peered inside at the gore—it was deformed, but it had not yet been pushed all the way into the form. It took three successive detonations to form each gore, but the technique it worked. The thin pie slices were carefully lifted from the water and set on a jig for safekeeping. What the residents of the bedroom communities near El Toro made of the 36 low-frequency explosions that rattled their homes is unknown.

SOLUTION:

Brainstorm: consider all ideas and inspirations, no matter how bizarre or unusual, because the answer may well be hiding in unexpected concepts.

Next, these wobbly, giant structures needed to be welded together to create the dome for the tank. The welds had to be perfect; even a tiny air bubble could cause a catastrophic crack at the temperatures the seams would encounter. When the S-II was being created in the early 1960s, such welds could be performed for a few feet, but nobody knew how to do it for the 22-foot length of the gores. The team had to invent a machine to do it. Again.

WELDING PAPER

It was like trying to weld tissue paper. First they had to support the gore in the proper orientation for welding. But the gores were so large and so thin that they sagged under their own weight. Ultimately someone hit upon the idea of holding them up with air pressure—inflating them, basically—preparatory to welding.

They created an arched scaffolding above the two gores and ran a welding machine along the track. This sounds simple; it was not. The machine had to have both a welding head and an x-ray machine to verify the perfection of the weld. Additionally, the whole assembly needed to be large enough to accommodate a live operator, and the welds needed to be accurate to damn near within microns.

Once completed, the two domes had to be sandwiched together. Again, the lower dome was held up via inflation. The phenolic material (the plastic honeycomb) was laid carefully onto the 33-foot-diameter dome with adhesives, then baked at 300°F. Then they lowered the other dome on top and repeated the process. To keep this second dome from deforming, they reversed the process used on the lower one and made a vacuum-powered "hat" that could suck on the dome, causing it to maintain its shape until it was lowered onto the sticky phenolic honeycomb. They then welded the two domes together at their edges like a giant aluminum calzone.

The structure was then lowered into the cylindrical hull and welded in place. Then the miles of wire, complex pumps and piping, and the five rocket engines would be added to the mix. The final result was as tall as three boxcars and as wide as one.

This was not an undertaking for the impatient or the faint of heart . . . nor was it a pleasant place for accountants. At one point, NAA management was tracking at least 30,000 separate processes. One manager walking the floor found a machinist working to shave microns from an intricate part—a part that had already been replaced by an updated design. Procedural rules allowed about a dozen changes to a drawing before it needed to be reviewed or replaced; this one had already had nearly a hundred, and the part that was being made was useless before it was finished. That was the kind of nightmare that the S-II process had become, and one that kept the accountants—and the managers—up at night.

DELIVERY AND DELIVERANCE

In 1967, as the S-II stages were finally arriving at Cape Canaveral for test flights, the *Apollo 1* fire occurred. This tragic event, detailed earlier in this book, killed the three astronauts who were training inside the Apollo capsule while it sat on the launchpad in Florida. Its pure oxygen environment caught fire and killed the trio almost instantaneously. In the congressional fiasco that followed, NASA and North American would each give up one of its own to appease the (allegedly) well-intentioned but hawkish legislators who were seeking "answers," or, more properly, someone to blame. For NASA, it would be a man named Joe Shea, Harrison Storms's opposite number in the space agency. For North American, it would be Storms. He would be gone when *Apollo 8* was launched in 1968. He was not even invited to the launch of *Apollo 11*, the first to land men on the moon. But he did view the liftoff from a friend's yacht not far from the launch facility. The cruel irony of it all was this: his was one of the few voices that had warned NASA about the folly of a pure oxygen environment in the Command Module many years before. But as so often occurs in great endeavors, those who are right do not necessarily win the day.

As *Apollo 11* rose into the crystalline blue sky, Storms leaned against the boat's railing. He could picture some of the millions of components that were hard at work taking three men to the moon. He also knew that his personal stamp—brash, aggressive, and daring—was all over the hardware that was making its way into orbit. Somehow that made it all worthwhile.

INNOVATIONS

- Evolved the use of a large and lightweight "common bulkhead" design in a cryogenic rocket stage to save weight.
- Won multiple challenging Apollo bids, changing the course of business development at North American.
- Invented new techniques for processes that had not even been envisioned before. production of the S-II, such as

mobile welding robots and explosive forming of large metal parts.

- Designed and built one of the most advanced flying structures in history, with the same design efficiency as an eggshell.
- Managed to keep the S-II design sufficiently fluid to accommodate continual changes in the first stage, the third stage, and the LM and Command Module by NASA.
- Designed a successful compromise among weight, power, and rigidity for safe operations with no in-flight failures.

CHAPTER 10

A DARING GAMBIT: *APOLLO 8*

CHALLENGES

- Man-rate a launcher after only two tests, both of which had several issues.
- Build consensus for a daring, last-minute change in mission plans.
- Shift crew personnel in the middle of extensive and specialized training.
- Prepare Mission Control personnel for a far earlier flight to the moon than anticipated.
- Calculate acceptable odds for mission success—a life-or-death proposition.

NOT CLOSE TO READY

As if James Webb, the embattled NASA administrator, was not under enough pressure after the *Apollo 1* fire, top-secret memos like this one crossed his desk with distressing regularity. JFK had given NASA the task of buoying American global prestige by landing a man on the moon before the Soviet Union did, and by the end of the decade. The Soviets, for their part, had regularly beaten the

> TOP SECRET
> 2 March 1967
> NATIONAL INTELLIGENCE ESTIMATE
> Number 11-1-67
>
> SUBJECT: THE SOVIET SPACE PROGRAM
> [Handle via indicated controls]
>
> SUMMARY:
> The number of space launches attempted in the past two years was nearly equal to the total of the preceding seven years. . . .
>
> A continuing high level of development activity and construction of major new launch facilities suggest that a new series of advanced space missions is likely in the next few years. . . .
>
> [The Soviets] have tested a new booster with a thrust of 2.5 to 3 million pounds. . .
>
> They are building a major new launch facility at Tyuratam that will be able to take vehicles with a first-stage thrust in the 8,000,000–16,000,000 pound range. . . .
>
> The Soviets will probably attempt a manned circumlunar flight during the next two years.

pants off the United States with spectacular space firsts. Since the Kennedy directive, NASA had been doggedly plugging away at the Apollo program, but had suffered setbacks that included the fire in February of 1967 and now a Lunar Module and Saturn V second stage that were falling dangerously behind schedule. Webb was not a happy man.

Out in Downey, California, Frank Borman was not a happy man, either. Since the accident that killed three of his fellow astronauts on the pad, Borman had been out at the North American Aviation plant where the Apollo capsule and Service Module (the life support and rocket unit behind it) were being fabricated. When he got there, he was not pleased with what he saw—and he let everyone know it, both through "proper channels" and by reporting directly to the top.

When Borman entered the room, you did not need to see him—you *felt* him. A bit of the air was sucked out, and it became immediately clear that a profound entity had taken root nearby. But it was not just ego; it was a commanding presence. Borman stood out as a patriot in an astronaut corps that was filled with patriots. God, duty, country—that was his honest-to-goodness motto. And woe be to anyone who tried to stand in his way.

Just shy of his fortieth birthday, Borman had already left a mark on NASA. A short, scrappy West Point man, he had had a brief career as a fighter pilot before joining NASA. Borman had flown the *Gemini 7* mission and had been NASA's selection to represent the astronaut corps during the *Apollo 1* investigations. In the latter role, Borman excelled. He was painfully honest and direct in his testimony, sometimes not in a way that flattered NASA. He had wrapped up the occasionally brutal congressional proceedings in a fashion that probably went a long way toward saving Apollo. When asked how the astronauts felt about the dangers they faced, he opened a letter written some months before by the recently deceased Gus Grissom and read it in a tone that only hinted at the emotions he was surely feeling. The note made it clear that Grissom had appreciated the dangers that faced them and wanted the program to continue no matter what. Then, when asked for his personal recommendation, Borman stated flatly to stop the "witch hunt" and get on with Apollo. That stark advice from a hero-astronaut had gone a long way toward ending the congressional raking over of the smoldering shell of *Apollo 1*.

Now, just months later, he was presiding over the redesign of the Apollo capsule. It was coming along nicely, which was more than you could say for the lunar module over at Grumman. In stark contrast, the LM, admittedly a more extreme and exotic design than even the capsule, was a mess. It was overweight, was prone to cracks in its paper-thin hull, and had a balky ascent engine, which was critical to its returning from the moon. None of these things could be hurried past a certain point, and all were critical to success.

But "success," for better or worse, meant landing on the moon by the end of 1969 (technically, the end of 1970 was the decade mark for Kennedy's challenge, but nobody thought of it that way). With the deadline less than 18 months away, NASA had to keep to a schedule—and the LM was knocking it to hell.

Nonetheless, NASA was preparing for the launch of *Apollo 7*, the first flight of the new and improved Apollo capsule, which was slated for October 1968. For this flight only, the capsule would be launched without an LM on the older, less powerful Saturn 1B rocket. If all went well, Borman was to lead his crew in *Apollo 8*, which would use the Saturn V and carry an LM into Earth orbit for extensive testing. He was as excited about that mission as he ever got about anything. To his crewmates, when Colonel Borman got excited, he merely got more ornery. But he was good at what he did—nobody would debate that.

AN URGENT CALL

One Saturday, an urgent call was transferred to his temporary work area at the North American plant. Borman assumed that it was just another nuisance call from NASA headquarters. It was a hot August weekend in southern California, and the air conditioning at the plant—such as it was—did little to keep up with the intense heat. Borman was already edgy and did not need interference from the top. When he was told that the call was from Deke Slayton, head of the astronaut office, he became more perplexed than irritated. At least Deke was a former astronaut, and he cut through the bullshit—it must be important.

"Frank, get back to Houston right away. I need to talk to you," Slayton barked.

"Talk to me *now*, Deke; I'm busy!" retorted Borman.

"I can't do this over the phone. Grab a plane and get back here," said Slayton with finality.

Deke was much like Frank: a no-nonsense, get-to-the-point kind of guy. Borman knew he had to get to Houston, so he did.

When he got to Slayton's office, Deke told him a story that was fantastic in its scope and implications. It was a tale of boldness, vision, and . . . danger. It ended with a question, and Borman had said yes to the assignment without even checking with his *Apollo 8* crewmates.

In short, the story went like this: since early 1967, the Soviets had been dealing with their own *Apollo 1*–type issues: *Soyuz 1* had had big problems during reentry, killing the lone cosmonaut. It was an amazing bit of timing, following the Apollo fire by three months. Both the United States' and the Soviet Union's lunar programs had been slow to recover. But while the issues with both the Apollo and the Soyuz capsules were being ironed out, the rockets—the U.S. Saturn V and the Russian rockets—moved aggressively forward.

The CIA reports and other top-secret documents showed a troubling trend. The Russians were refining their midsized booster while continuing work on a larger Saturn V–class rocket. The problem was that the Soviet program was so secretive—it operated under the Russian military—that little was known beyond (1) what was trumpeted (only after a successful mission) in the state-run newspaper *TASS* and (2) what was visible to the U.S. Corona satellites as they slowly gathered visual evidence from their distant orbits high above. But this indirect evidence was what had the CIA, and, by extension, NASA, so worried.

And there was more. The Soviets had also flown a series of unmanned missions that they called *Zond*, which was simply Russian for "probe." How innocuous. The first three had been just that: unmanned probes. But then in March of 1968, they lofted *Zond 4*, and this time it was a modified unmanned Soyuz spacecraft, clearly experimenting with round-the-moon trajectories. *Zond 5* would follow months later. Between them, they tested the ability to leave low Earth orbit, reenter at high speeds, engage in glancing reentries (which allowed the craft to skip off the atmosphere once before reentry, lowering the crushing g-forces experienced on high-speed lunar returns), and other activities that were critical to a lunar mission. Aboard each flight were experimental subjects—turtles, insects, and plants—to test any changes in tissues or metabolism from the journey. They even had tape-recorded messages from cosmonauts aboard to test the radio transmissions from deep space. Clearly they were preparing for something big, and most of the U.S. top brass feared that it could only be to beat Apollo to the moon.

The reasoning went like this: the Soviet space program was nowhere near ready to *land* a man on the moon; in fact, the Soviets were well behind the already lagging United States in that respect. Nor did they have a large enough rocket to send a Soyuz into orbit around the moon—yet. But they did have the smaller Proton booster, which could toss the Soyuz into a looping lunar flyby. And that was the exact trajectory that *Zond 5* flew in September 1968. If there was a *Zond 6*—a *manned* flyby of the moon—it would steal NASA's thunder; the clock was ticking.

Meanwhile, unmanned testing with the Apollo hardware also moved ahead. *Apollo 4* had flown without a crew in November of 1967, and while it was generally successful, it did point up some issues with the Saturn V that needed to be ironed out. Then *Apollo 5* flew in January 1968 on the smaller Saturn 1B. It was the first test of the lunar module, which was still too heavy to land on the moon. There were a number of other issues, including the fact that the windows on the LM tended to blow out at altitude. But the program soldiered on, with the unmanned *Apollo 6* flight in April of the same year. Another Saturn V flight, this one had terrible problems, including multiple engine failures in the second and third stages. The Germans in Huntsville sequestered themselves and applied their substantial talents, in their ordered and methodical way, to solving the problems. In just a matter of weeks, they had.

CHALLENGE:

To reach the moon before JFK's deadline, and especially before the Soviet Union, even with the Lunar Module dangerously behind schedule.

But in the meantime, the brass at the Johnson Space Center (JSC) was watching with concern as the Soviets seemed to be priming for something big. It would be in character for them to stage a space spectacular soon, and looping the moon would be the one to try. It would merely fly one big figure-eight path from the Earth to the moon and back, far less of a challenge than the manned landing the United States had applied itself to. But in the public mind, the Russians would have reached the moon and won the race—and that was simply not acceptable.

Nobody was more aware of the stakes than George Low. He had been with NASA since its formation and was an old hand at these things. As the manager of the Apollo Spacecraft Program Office, Low was privy to just about everything that was going on, both in the United States and what little was known about the USSR. He did not like what he saw.

While Low was a fan of process and the complex management program that NASA used to move Apollo to fruition, he was also a frequent critic of the approach to testing that the German team in

Huntsville used. He felt that the Germans were being too conservative and wasting time and resources. A few months earlier, Low had forced von Braun to skip many of his preferred increments and move to what Low called "all-up" testing, where you just built the whole rocket and shot it up, loaded with cameras and telemetry, to see if everything worked. No first-stage tests, then second-stage tests, and so on. Just build it and go. Low's approach worked, and brilliantly. Up to twelve tests had been boiled down to two or three, and it was estimated that up to a year had been shaved off the program.

Low now had a new vision. He knew that the Soviets were up to something. He was also enough of a politician to see that NASA in general and Apollo in particular were losing ground in the United States when it came to popular support. And as popular support goes, so goes political support. In January, U.S. forces had barely turned back Communist troops in the Tet Offensive in Vietnam, and that war was a shambles. By April 1968, Martin Luther King was dead, and in June Bobby Kennedy had also been assassinated. It was shaping up to be a rotten year, and Low knew that NASA could not afford to be second to the moon. It could be the end of the program.

In keeping with his aggressive approach, he came up with a suggestion that was met with a mixture of shock, surprise, and glee depending on whom he was speaking with. On Wednesday, August 7, 1968, Low met with Chris Kraft, the director of flight operations at JSC. They discussed the bottleneck of the tardy Lunar Module and other issues that were dogging the progress of the program. With no LM to test in flight, the *Apollo 8* Earth orbital mission would be in most ways just a repeat of *Apollo 7*. The only difference would be that they would be flying into orbit on top of a Saturn V instead of the 1B. But nothing new of real value would be accomplished. So what, Kraft asked, did Low have in mind?

A CHANGE OF PLANS

Low smiled as he dropped his bombshell: let's stop screwing around and fly *Apollo 8* into lunar orbit.

> **SOLUTION:**
>
> Compress the schedule, streamline testing, and be bold—go for the moon.

After Kraft recovered, he was enthusiastic about the idea. But both men knew that they had to tread carefully—there would be opposition. They engaged in a bit of cloak-and-dagger, setting up meetings with carefully selected individuals of importance within the program and keeping everyone else in the dark. Even the few files they kept were code-named, and their secretaries were told to keep them in "007" (for James Bond) mode. For some weeks, they didn't even tell Jim Webb, the NASA administrator. They wanted to make sure that they had everyone onboard before going to the top. That's when Low had asked Slayton to bring Borman in for a chat to ask him if he would like to take *Apollo 8* to the moon. Borman did not ponder the question or consult with his crew. He just said yes, then had to think of a way to break the news to his long-suffering wife. She took it like a trouper, but she later admitted that she thought the odds for success—and survival—were 50-50 at best.

> **CHALLENGE:**
>
> How to calculate the statistical—and acceptable—risk for a flight with little redundancy in case of emergency.

The plan to send *Apollo 8* to the moon was brash, bold, daring, and dangerous. At the core of the decision were statistical odds.

The Lunar Module had always been considered a potential lifeboat should something go wrong with the Apollo capsule or the Service Module that powered it. Without the LM, should the CSM engine not fire up to break them free once they were in lunar orbit, they would be there to stay. As one astronaut put it, "We would be a permanent monument to NASA" in orbit around the moon. There was simply no redundancy, and that was something that NASA hated—the engineers liked there to be at least two ways to carry out any step in the flight. Statistical tyranny glowered at *Apollo 8*—there was a substantial risk of a mission-critical failure.

In short order, Low had met with everyone he needed to at the Manned Space Flight Center. Then the following Friday, only two days after he had approached Kraft, Low flew off to Huntsville to sound out von Braun. Von Braun and his team at Marshall had been laboring tirelessly over the issues with the Saturn V after the horrible *Apollo 6* test flight. They would need to be on board for this skullduggery to work, as Low was suggesting that they fly the spacecraft all the way out to the moon and back on the Saturn V's maiden voyage with a crew. There was much trepidation over what the conservative German might say.

SOLUTION:

Past a certain point, don't rely on statistical analysis. Outline the stakes, explain the risks, and then let the crew members—those whose lives are on the line—decide for themselves.

Von Braun was quickly swept up in the idea. It was, despite its brashness, the core of what he had been striving toward since 1938: reaching a new world. He joined the cabal. They all knew they had to get moving to make the deadline, and even those who were not privy to specific CIA reports knew that the Soviets were making advances weekly.

CONVINCING THE BOSS

A couple of days later, Tom Paine, who would soon replace Webb as NASA administrator, decided to play devil's advocate during one of the closed-door meetings about the new *Apollo 8* mission. He reminded the assembled engineers and managers that just weeks earlier, they had all been worried sick about the issues with the Saturn V booster tests. It was von Braun who had come up with the elegantly simple, though slightly chilling, reply: "Once you decide to man [a Saturn V], it doesn't matter how far you go." He could have added: "If there is a problem, the crew will be just as dead whether they're in Earth orbit or out by the moon." Each of them could arrive at his own conclusions.

Now all they had to do was convince the NASA administrator, James Webb. He was in Vienna at a conference, and thus it had been easy to bypass him as Low and his fellow conspirators quietly shopped the plan. On August 15, a week after the idea had been hatched, it was pitched to Webb.

His first reaction was not quite what they had hoped for. He fairly yelled into the phone: "Are you out of your minds?! You're putting our agency and the whole Apollo program at risk!" Webb was not enthusiastic.

But over the next couple of days, Webb thought the audacious plan over. He consulted with his CIA contacts. He looked over a write-up prepared by the plotters back in Houston. But there was more at stake here than mere risk analysis: Webb also knew that his days at NASA were numbered. LBJ's tenure as president was just about up, and he had announced back in March that he would not seek a second term. Webb would be out, and Paine would be the transitional NASA boss until an incoming presidential administration decided whom it wanted in charge. It was time for Webb to take a broader view, and perhaps consider something that would assure him a legacy beyond the overall Apollo program. This could be it. He agreed, albeit with some lingering reluctance.

And so the plan to not just fly *Apollo 8 past* the moon, but to enter lunar orbit and do at least 10 laps before coming home, was now official. Everything went into high gear: crews were reshuffled, training was intensified, and hardware was adjusted, inspected, and prepared. Perhaps the most pressure was on the Instrumentation Lab at MIT, where the software to fly to the moon and back had to be prepared, as the people there had not planned for this mission so early. The only folks who actually got a slight relief from the Apollo grind were those at Grumman, who now had a bit more time to complete the Lunar Module. But it was largely an illusion; the end of the decade was near enough to touch.

CHALLENGE:

Overcoming broader institutional aversion to risk.

Any remaining reticence over the daring mission evaporated when on September 14, the Russians launched their new Proton rocket again. The unmanned Soyuz moonship sped off to the moon, handily looping that world three days later at an altitude of 1,100 miles—not nearly as close as *Apollo 8* would get at 60 miles, but proof that the Soviets had also mastered the complexities of navigating beyond Earth orbit. On September 21, *Zond 5* splashed down in the Indian Ocean, and the Soviet press heralded the mission as a success. It had not been. NASA did not have all the facts, but the mission design dictated that the Soyuz capsule was supposed to include a skip-glide reentry path to scrub off g-forces, just as *Apollo 8* would do in a few months. *Zond 5* failed in that attempt, slamming straight into the Earth's atmosphere and enduring a bone-crushing

16 gs during reentry. The Soviets knew that they were losing valuable time in the race to reach the moon, but NASA—not being privy to the results of the flight—could not be sure where they stood. The lunar orbit plan for *Apollo 8* gained urgency.

In October of 1968, *Apollo 7* rose from Florida with three astronauts aboard. While it did not use the Saturn V as a booster, it was a complete test of everything aboard the Command and Service Modules except for the high-speed reentry that coming back from the moon would entail (that had already been tested in the unmanned flights). While the crew caught colds and got testy with Mission Control, the life support systems (so fretted over since the *Apollo 1* fire and redesign) and all the navigation and maneuvering systems worked just about perfectly. The mission was declared an unqualified success, and the Apollo spacecraft was declared ready to go to the moon.

SOLUTION:

Every tale of daring needs a challenge—or, as in this case, a villain: the Soviet Union. America's Cold War rival was the perfect lever for making bold decisions about Apollo.

That same month, the Soviets launched another Soyuz, but this time it was manned by a single cosmonaut and went only into Earth orbit. It suffered none of the malfunctions that had plagued *Soyuz 1*. The pilot conducted rendezvous tests with another Soyuz capsule that had been launched unmanned the previous day. Both craft landed successfully after apparently accomplishing the mission's stated goals. It was still going to be a close thing, this race to the moon.

With the USSR breathing down its neck, NASA still had a malfunctioning Saturn V to deal with. The engineers in Huntsville and their prime contractors—Boeing, North American, and McDonnell-Douglas—were working around the clock to get the booster sorted out. As it turned out, the entire structure of the first stage tended to resonate at a frequency close to that of the firing F-1 engines, and this could create destructive harmonics. Von Braun had his people continue to work on "detuning" the Saturn's first stage, which eventually solved the problem: the rocket would no longer be a skyscraper-sized tuning fork. Then there were the balky upper-stage engines—they were shutting down early, and sometimes not relighting as they would have to to head off to the moon. But the Huntsville team, working with Rocketdyne in California, licked that problem too, when it discovered a nasty tendency for a fuel line to vibrate itself to pieces as the rocket gained altitude. They removed a bellows and added some bends to the slim pipe—a remarkably tiny fix in the grand scheme of things. The Saturn V stack was soon declared ready to go, just as von Braun had promised it would be. The rocket never again had a major failure in flight.

The crew of *Apollo 8* continued to train frantically. The training schedule had been very tight, and now the flight was a matter of weeks away. Much still had to be learned and internalized if the crew was to succeed. Borman was the commander, Jim Lovell (who had flown a Gemini flight with Borman) was the navigator, and Bill Anders, a rookie, was the pilot. The other Apollo crews mostly took a break while these three worked continuously to prepare.

OVERCOMING DOUBT

This was the boldest mission that NASA had yet undertaken, and there were other skeptics within the Apollo upper management besides the departing Jim Webb. George Meuller, one of JSC's top brass, was edgy about the mission plan. As late as November of that year, he was requesting that they take one more long, objective look and carefully consider the risks versus the rewards of the moon trip. As he put it, "There are grave risks to the program as a whole, not just the *Apollo 8* mission," he wrote, "[and] you and I know that if failure comes, the reaction will be that 'anyone should have known better than to undertake such a trip at this point in time.'" Upper management was divided on the undertaking.

And Meuller was right. The mission as planned was a desperately risky thing, and failure would have been devastating to Apollo and NASA, coming just under two years after the fire. There were any number of bad things that could happen on the way out to the moon and back, and there would be no Lunar Module as a lifeboat to save them. The rocket engine on the Service Module was a single engine that had been used only once on a manned mission (*Apollo 7*), though it had been well tested in the unmanned flights of *Apollo 4* and *Apollo 6*. If for some reason the engine did not ignite after braking them into orbit around the moon (and after soaking in the cold of space for another full day), they would be stuck without hope of returning home. Then there were other systems that were critical: life support, maneuvering thrusters, the navigational computer, and many others. Some of these systems had redundancy built in, but even that could fail. With well over a million parts and 15 miles of wire in the Command Module alone, there was plenty that could go wrong, and no single part of the system had been tested in space more than three times. It was a slim margin upon which three lives would depend.

In the final review with the contractors, only McDonnell-Douglas went on record with a contrary vote. McDonnell supported going to the moon, but wanted to conduct a figure-eight flyby instead of entering orbit. This was interesting, since McDonnell had built only the third stage of the booster and had had nothing to do with the systems that were critical for bringing Apollo home—its S-IVB would be discarded upon leaving Earth orbit. But that was the company's recommendation—its people were nervous. North American, the builder of the second stage and the Command and Service Modules, and whose Rocketdyne division was responsible for the SM's rocket engine and upper-stage engines, were confident in their hardware. The plan moved ahead despite McDonnell's reservations.

Nudging the doubters toward agreement was a great deal of psychological momentum around the mission, which was fed by the grim news coming in a continual stream from the CIA and other sources regarding the Soviets. It was, in management's minds, now or never.

The morning of December 21, 1968, was typically chilly for winter at the Cape. The astronauts arose at 3 a.m. to get ready; George Low met them for breakfast to see off the men whose lives he was gambling in this (his) mission. The trio soon made the trek out to the pad and up to the capsule atop the frosty, mist-enshrouded rocket. Just before 8 a.m., the fog turned to smoke as the titanic machine thundered off the pad and into space. After a few orbits and systems checks, they got the word: "Apollo 8, you are go for TLI [trans-lunar injection]."

In the wee hours of the morning on December 24, they reached the moon. There had been a few tense moments on the ground during the journey that the astronauts never knew about. As they were hurtling away from Earth, someone in upper management suddenly got cold feet about the navigational mathematics being used by ground control. These numbers had been created and checked by many of the finest mathematicians and celestial navigation experts on Earth. They had been run through the enormous computers of the day time and time again, and had been checked and rechecked. The plans had even been used to send robotic orbiters and landers to the moon for many years—yet now, some people were nervous. The night before the spacecraft was set to make orbit around the moon, an engineer working in one of the "back rooms" that supported mission control was surprised when Apollo's top brass—Meuller,

Gilruth, and Kraft—came into his office with urgent looks on their faces. "How sure are you that we are going to *miss the moon*??" one of them asked. He replied, "I am real sure." The three managers left, and the engineer had a good laugh. He thought it was a hell of a time for them to get nervous about years of calculations and worry that *Apollo 8* might slam into the moon.

Daring by definition is rarely easy or without fear.

Seventy hours after launch, the spacecraft disappeared behind the moon. Communications ceased, as everyone knew they would. How long it took for them to be reestablished would tell Mission Control whether or not the spacecraft's engine had fired and burned long enough to slow them into orbit around the moon. Then, within a second of when it was predicted, the radio signal came down from *Apollo 8*—all was well. They were in lunar orbit.

Staying for 10 orbits, the crew spent Christmas Eve conducting observations until it was time for them to sign off. Then, to commemorate the holiday, they delivered a closing message that would become one of the most historic of the entire space age. Taking turns, each man read a section from Genesis, and Borman finished with, "And from the crew of Apollo 8, we close with goodnight, good luck, a Merry Christmas, and God bless all of you, all of you on the good Earth." Tears were shed in Mission Control that night.

BOLDNESS REWARDED

After the tenth and hopefully final orbit, *Apollo 8* disappeared behind the moon, as it had done nine times since its arrival. Once again Mission Control sweated out the wait. But this time it was different. When Borman, Lovell, and Anders first arrived at the moon, had the rocket not fired, they would have swung into a free-return trajectory and come back home. Now if the rocket failed to fire, they would stay there until they died of asphyxiation. The minutes dragged by.

And then, right on time, came Jim Lovell's voice: "Please be informed, there is a Santa Claus." The engine had fired, and *Apollo 8* was coming home.

Up in the capsule, Borman was exhausted but happy. The mission had gone off without a hitch. He had met all mission objectives to his satisfaction, although he had curtailed some activities and cut others short because of his conservative nature. Get there, make orbit, stay as briefly as possible, and then come home. These had been his goals. While Lovell and Anders had been almost giddy while they were in lunar orbit, Borman stayed stoic until almost the last minute. And now he was just damned happy to be coming home.

Just under three days later, an exhausted but happy crew left their spacecraft as it bobbed in calm seas near a U.S. Navy carrier. The mission was over, and within 10 weeks *Apollo 9* would launch, an Earth-orbital mission that would test the much delayed Lunar Module. But Frank Borman had decided that enough was enough, and that he was leaving active flight status to pursue other adventures within NASA and beyond. He was eventually asked to serve as liaison to the White House during the *Apollo 11* mission, and he also followed the life-or-death drama of *Apollo 13* while working on special projects within the space agency. Soon he would depart from NASA to become CEO of Eastern Air Lines.

But Borman paid special attention to the drama of *Apollo 13*. Jim Lovell, the commander of that mission, was his Gemini and Apollo crewmate and a close personal friend. When the oxygen tank in the Service Module exploded, the lives of the three astronauts onboard were in grave danger. Only the fact that they could move over to the Lunar Module for the remainder of the mission saved their lives. Now, had that oxygen tank from *Apollo 13*'s Service Module instead been installed in *Apollo 8*'s Service Module—well, Borman was not the kind of person to dwell on such things. He was more concerned about seeing the boys on *Apollo 13* home safe and sound.

But George Low and many others surely took pause. All the daring and bravado that it took to send *Apollo 8* around the moon and beat the Soviets in that decade-long race would have been for naught had *Apollo 8* had the same difficulties as *Apollo 13* at the same time in the trip. They could easily have had that oxygen tank on *Apollo 8*'s Service Module, and with no LM to succor them, the crew would have been dead before they reached the moon. The likely outcomes: burning up in a botched reentry, skipping off the atmosphere, or returning to Earth as three asphyxiated corpses. The news coverage of Navy frogmen retrieving the dead bodies from a bobbing Command Module would probably have ended the Apollo program, if not NASA itself.

But that didn't happen. And, in the words of the philosopher/theologian Norman Vincent Peale, "First, be bold, and mighty forces will come to your aid." Whether by luck, fate, or just good old engineering skill, *Apollo 8*'s daring journey had been a rousing success.

INNOVATIONS:

- Compression of von Braun's conservative, step-by-step rocket testing program by initiating "all-up" testing, where the entire rocket and all its components were tested at once.
- Convincing an engineering-based organization that made decisions based on quantifiable data and statistics to listen, at least in part, to its heart.
- A sufficiently flexible and robust system of crew selection and training that could accommodate last-minute changes in flight plans and crew assignments, along with complex mission preparation.

- Designed-in redundancies in both hardware and procedures to maximize the chances of success.
- Rapid analysis of risk versus reward in the face of Soviet advances and skeptical peers.

CHAPTER 11

APOLLO 11: CENTER OF GRAVITY

CHALLENGES

- To train a cadre of engineers, flight controllers, technicians, managers, and, most important, astronauts to perform during a great leap into the unknown: the first manned landing on the moon.
- Given an almost total lack of practical experience and only two moon-orbital reconnaissance flights, identify the best methods of teaching your ground and flight crews how to cope with an almost limitless number of potential disasters.
- Learn how to control a mission from the Earth that is taking place 250,000 miles away.

SIMULATING DISASTER

The mission of *Apollo 11*, the first crewed spacecraft to land on the moon, benefited from a huge advance pioneered by NASA in the early 1960s: training and simulation. This was a refinement of the type of training pioneered by the U.S. military in the 1930s and 1940s. A machine called the Link Simulator was designed to train large numbers of pilots in the intricacies of flying. Only 20 years later, digital computers were simulating complex lunar missions, interfacing with both the astronauts and ground controllers with a high degree of realism.

CHALLENGE:

Train astronauts and flight controllers—while on the ground—to make split-second, mission-critical decisions during flight.

In the Mission Operations Control Room in Houston from which American space flights were managed, and from spacecraft simulators in Florida, fictional missions to the moon were flown (and crashed) almost daily. The astronauts would climb into a mock-up of a capsule that was connected via computer and human interfaces to the control room being used for that exercise. Then, with the trainees on both ends of the system, the simulation supervisors, known as SimSups (or "those dirty bastards," depending on your mood that day), worked invisibly between them, throwing carefully designed monkey wrenches into the works. It was unnerving and exasperating, but it was effective—and for the first lunar landing, probably lifesaving. *Apollo* astronauts would frequently credit their exhaustive training for the success of their missions.

SOLUTION:

Invent a mediated training system that simulates entire missions in high-realism conditions. Use it mercilessly until hesitation is adapted out.

THE GIANT LEAP

July 20, 1969: It had been just a couple of hours since Neil Armstrong and Buzz Aldrin had climbed into the Lunar Module *Eagle*, sealed the hatch, and separated from the Command Module (in which Mike Collins would wait, alone and anxious for his comrades, for the next 20 hours). Yet already Armstrong, the mission commander, knew that they had problems. For some reason they were not where they wanted to be as they descended to the moon's surface, and that bothered his regimented pilot's mind.

Neil and Buzz stood in the Lunar Module—there were no seats, nor was there any need for them in the one-sixth gravity of the moon. They were suspended from the ceiling by straps, and this standing position allowed them a splendid view out the front windows. But right now that view was bothersome, because if he was reading the alignment marks etched on the glass correctly, they were coming in "long," meaning that they would overshoot their landing site in the Sea of Tranquility. NASA would later hypothesize that a tiny bit of residual air in the tunnel between the Apollo capsule and the Lunar Module, as well as a few thruster firings, had given the LM a bit of extra kick when the two had separated, which was enough to send them miles downrange. Spaceflight is a tricky business.

> **CHALLENGE:**
>
> When ground-based simulations are not enough, how do you train for a lunar landing?

Armstrong had experience landing on the moon . . . in theory. Besides the hundreds of hours in the "static" or unmoving "Lunar Module" simulator, NASA had invented a very convincing—and incredibly dangerous—flyer for training use on Earth. It was called the Lunar Landing Research Vehicle, or LLRV. In essence, it was a framework with legs surrounding a large, howling jet engine that was pointed straight down. The thrust from this engine removed five-sixths of the device's weight, leaving just enough downward velocity to feel like a lunar lander hovering over the moon. The engine was throttlable across a range from that 20 percent gravitational tug to zero. To the sides of the frame were little jets that allowed control just like the LM, and strapped into an ejection seat dangling out front was the pilot.

SOLUTION:

Design a machine that flies—on Earth—much the way the Lunar Module does in the one-sixth gravity of the moon. Use this exhaustively for training the LM pilot.

Three of the machines had been lost to crashes, and Armstrong had been at the controls during the scariest of them. During a routine simulation, the jet engine had swung off-center—it was mounted on a gimbal—and jammed there. The LLRV began to veer to one side. If it went too far over, it would slide into the ground in a heartbeat; he would have no chance to eject.

True to form, the icy-cool Armstrong rode it until the very last second, ejecting just as the machine fell sideways into the tarmac and exploded in a huge ball of orange flame. Training indeed. But despite the dangers, Armstrong was grateful to the LLRV—he felt that of all the lunar landing simulations, it was the most convincing.

DESCENDING

Armstrong and Aldrin continued toward the moon. Back on the ground at Mission Control, Gene Kranz, the 36-year-old flight director during the *Apollo 11* landing phase, paced behind his row of consoles. Of medium height and build, he looked both pugnacious, with his Marine Corps crew cut and ramrod-straight bearing, and resplendent, in his gaudy white-brocade vest. His wife made him a new, customized vest for each mission, and this one made him look like a bleached matador. But he was the Boss, a true steely-eyed missile man, the guy who listened to John Phillips Sousa marches every morning to get revved up, so nobody dared laugh at his adornments. Kranz had not just earned his stripes in Mission Control—he was an early protégé of Chris Kraft—but had quite literally written the spaceflight rule book under Kraft's command. When Kranz cited or violated a flight rule, it was his to observe or break. In most cases, he had invented it.

CHALLENGE:

How to select candidates for flight controllers—who must make split-second, life-critical decisions—for an unknown set of challenges.

Below Kranz's station spread two more rows of consoles made famous by a decade of space race TV broadcasts. His row made the third, and there was one behind him for NASA's top brass. Below him, young flight controllers sat before the primitive computer screens, spaced about three feet apart. At these consoles, they listened to the flight chatter through clunky headphones, flipped fat switches, and punched wide, lit buttons on the control panels. It was all very *Star Trek*.

Kranz was more intense than nervous. They had trained for this for years, endured the suspenseful moon orbital flight of *Apollo 8*, watched and listened as the Lunar Module of *Apollo 10* made a low pass at the moon's surface before coming home (with a tense moment when the craft temporarily spun out of control), and now they were running the first landing attempt. He had faith in his flight controllers—young men whose average age was just 26. "I wanted people young enough to not know failure," Kranz would later say, "and they were *my* people."

SOLUTION:

Select from the best, brightest . . . and youngest. As Gene Kranz, Apollo flight director, said: "I wanted people young enough to not know failure."

INSPIRATION BEFORE DANGER

Before the landing had begun, Kranz ordered the doors locked and the circuit breakers blocked into place. This was no time for a crazed intruder or random electrical failure. He then gave a short address that was not recorded but said: "OK, gang, we are really going to go and land on the moon today. That's no bullshit; we are going to land on the moon. We are about to do something that no one has ever done. Be aware that there is a lot of stuff that we don't know about the environment that we are about to walk into, but also know that I trust each of you implicitly. But I'm also aware that we are all human. So somewhere along the line, if we have a problem, I am here to take the heat for you. We are working in an area of the unknown that has high risk, but we don't even think of tying this game, we think only to win." He spoke a bit more, and finished with, "After we finish this sonofagun, we'll go out, have a beer and say 'Damnit, *we really did something*.'" It was vintage Kranz, and it worked. His crew was galvanized. No pregame coach's rant ever did better.

Soon his mind was split between Houston and 240,000 miles away near the lunar surface. With only a scratchy radio connection to go by, he was trying to picture what was going on up there.

He had just given the go for PDI, or powered descent initiation. In the acronym-laden jargon of NASA, it was a way of saying that Armstrong and Aldrin were go to attempt a landing. The two astronauts had responded and fired the LM's engine, beginning the long fall toward the silent, rocky surface below them. And then the trouble started.

Communication was spotty. This had, of course, all been simulated time and again by the sadistic SimSups, but this time it was for real, and the simulated solutions were not helping. At a controller's suggestion, Aldrin adjusted the antenna on the LM and that seemed to help—for a while. But the radio link with the crew was sporadic. However, the telemetry—the flow of technical data from the sensors aboard the LM—was adequate, so he decided to continue the landing. But if it got any worse, he would order an abort and bring them home.

CHALLENGE:

Prepare your trained team for all possible problems and outcomes—even those you have not yet thought of.

He was acutely aware that an abort was a possibility—this was, after all, the first time anyone had tried to land on another world—but he dreaded it. It would mean separating the LM's top and bottom stages and firing the ascent engine, all within seconds, just a few dozen feet above the lunar surface. This procedure had been practiced in the safety of Earth orbit once, but below a certain altitude over the moon, nobody was really sure if it would work or if an abort would simply result in a few acres of shredded aluminum foil and two dead astronauts. To add to this stress, last week's simulations had been particularly brutal. Usually the SimSups took it easy on flight controllers in the weeks before a major mission milestone like this one, but someone had decided to slip a little-known computer error into the simulation. When the alarm flashed on the flight controller's consoles, nobody knew what the hell it was—the little onboard navigation computer, critical to the landing, was protesting that it was overloaded with work and might quit at any time. Steve Bales, the controller on the relevant console, had never seen the alarm code before—nobody had—and aborted the simulated landing. As it turned out, the alarm had been noncritical, and Bales had scratched a (simulated) billion-dollar moon mission on a mistaken call. The post-sim briefing had not been pleasant, and Kranz's people had doubled down to make sure that it would not happen again. But now that event was forgotten for the moment. They were landing for real today.

SOLUTION:

Use clever simulation design to train mercilessly for every conceivable challenge. Then, to address unknown ones, encourage bold decision making and adapt out fear.

"COMPUTER ALARM . . ."

Up in the LM, Armstrong was concentrating hard on his instruments. They were now flying backside down and legs first, the LM windows looking up into empty space so that the rear-pointing radar could "see" the moon. The engine had been firing for about six minutes, but it seemed like forever. Communications with Houston were still drifting in and out. Their radar had acquired the range to the surface, seen that they were a bit high in altitude, and started adjusting the attitude to compensate. Then, on the small numeric computer display, a perplexing message came up. This screen was always a pattern of letters and numbers, usually calling out range or altitude. But this readout was weird—the display locked up and read just four numbers: 1202. The number glared like an accusation.

Aldrin looked at it, then looked over at Neil, who just flicked a glance at the screen, and then Armstrong called down to Mission Control with no discernable concern, just a firm tone: "Computer alarm."

In Mission Control, backs stiffened and eyeballs snapped to their consoles. Then Armstrong continued, "It's a 1202." The controllers looked confused—not a feeling they were accustomed to. A few voices inquired, "What the hell is a 1202?" to nobody in particular. Then all eyes went to Bales's console, the man responsible for deciphering the alarm and making a decision. Kranz held off, but everyone knew that he wanted an answer, and right now. Bales broke into a sweat, but Jack Garmin, Bales's backroom support, recalled the relevant simulation and had a cheat-sheet of codes ready. The 1202 alarm was an obscure software debugging code and should not be popping up in flight.

Armstrong's voice, getting impatient, crackled over the speakers at the top of the Big Board again: "Give us a reading on that computer alarm." There was no panic, and barely a hint of strain . . . but it was not a request.

Garmin and Bales understood that for some reason the computer thought it was getting too much data. It was signaling that the data overflow was getting critical and that it might shut down and start over. But so long as the alarm did not persist, it should be OK. "We're go on that, flight," Bales said. "If it doesn't reoccur, we're still go." Kranz nodded and acknowledged, "Rog" (short for "Roger"). The 36-year-old flight director had taken the advice of a 26-year-old controller who had been advised by a 24-year-old electronics tech. It was a day for young men to make decisions.

Down at the CapCom console sat Charlie Duke, a fellow astronaut who had flown Gemini and would soon copilot his own moon landing. CapCom was the only one allowed to speak to the astronauts during critical stages of the mission—it had been this way since Mercury, as the managers realized that pilots wanted to talk to other pilots in moments of stress. Duke cleared his throat and said, "Roger, we got you. We are go on that alarm."

CHALLENGE:

How to best assist seasoned test-pilot astronauts 240,000 miles away as they encounter dangerous situations.

It was at that point that an idea that had been forming in Kranz's mind during the last few years coalesced. The center of gravity—or, more precisely, the center of decision-making power—had just shifted out toward the moon. He and his controllers may have just made one of the last meaningful decisions of the landing phase—that the computer alarm was OK, they were still go. Now they would be able to monitor the landing via telemetry and audio (when it worked) and give suggestions and offer occasional advice, but the real authority had shifted out into space, and rested in the hands of Neil Armstrong. It was not a feeling that Kranz liked, but he was resigned to it. He gripped his pencil until his hand began to hurt. He had just seen an example of how extensive training had paid off for his controllers, and he hoped to hell that it would be the same for the crew up there, struggling to land in a hostile and largely unknown environment.

SOLUTION:

Learn when to let go. Decide when the "center of gravity" of decision making has gone "into the field"; let the person on-site make his own decisions; and support him as well as you can.

As they reached the 3,000-foot mark, Kranz polled his controllers: were they go for landing? To a man they responded in the affirmative, so Kranz made the call: go for landing. It was his final act of authority before touchdown. CapCom Duke had no sooner passed up the good news, when Aldrin spoke: "Program alarm, 1201." This time Bales said quickly, "Same type; we're go." The word was passed up to the crew.

The program alarms would sound for the rest of the landing, but the technicians had made the right call. These alarms did not ultimately affect the mission other than causing some sweaty palms and skipped heartbeats. But now a new problem reared its head.

CRUNCH TIME

As Aldrin monitored the speed and altitude readouts, Armstrong concentrated on the view outside the window. He did not like what he saw. The computer was bringing them down right into a field of truck-sized boulders. Armstrong took manual control. He had never really planned to let the computer land the LM anyway; no *real* pilot would. He began searching—rapidly—for a clearing.

In Mission Control, an indicator lit on the consoles: "ATT HOLD," or attitude hold. This was not good—it meant that Armstrong was no longer descending but had arrested downward motion and was flying forward in a hover, using copious amounts of precious fuel. The graph from orbit to landing was supposed to be, in general, a simple slope to touchdown, but it was now tapering dangerously.

On the ground, Kranz wondered what Armstrong was up to but, as a former USMC pilot himself, he knew that it was best to trust his astronauts. His team on the ground had done its bit, ably aided by extensive training and simulation. They would soon learn how it worked for the pilots in the LM.

With 100 feet remaining, the ground loop had gone largely silent. All that was heard now was Aldrin's recitation of the readouts and a controller's call that everyone knew was coming: "Low level." This referred to fuel, which was becoming dangerously low.

CHALLENGE:

In a split second, make a life-or-death decision on scanty data and information—and instinct.

The mission—and NASA's future—was in Armstrong's hands now. The next call came: "60 seconds." The room got very tense, very quiet. In one minute they needed to either be on the surface or hit the abort switch. Nobody wanted the latter.

But the procedure was theoretical; for obvious reasons, nobody had tried the maneuver at this low an altitude before. It might or might not work. They might ascend to safety, or they might crash before the ascent stage could gain altitude.

SOLUTION:

Combine training, experience, and your gut feeling to make a decision, and quickly.

"Thirty seconds," said Charlie Duke—less than a half-minute of fuel remained before a required abort, according to the readouts. Aldrin gave a terse acknowledgement; Armstrong was concentrating on the surface just 30 feet below. There was so much dust flying that he could not see the LM's landing pads, nor could he see the ground below very well, but he knew that it was there. And, better still, it was relatively flat.

A long sensor jutting from a landing leg touched the lunar surface, and a blue light on the console came on. "Contact light," Aldrin said flatly. The LM descended the last few feet, thumping to an abrupt stop on the moon. The two fatigued but elated astronauts stood there for a moment, stunned. They were down, with about 20 seconds of fuel showing on the gauges.

In Mission Control, the controllers sat tensely, most of them barely breathing. Soon the memorable words came down from the LM—Armstrong, talking in unruffled, almost laconic tones, said: "Houston, Tranquility Base here . . . the *Eagle* has landed."

Cheers erupted throughout the control center. Kranz realized that he was shaking, and looked down at his right hand. He had snapped the pencil he was holding, and his palm was deeply indented. With a small grin he let the pieces drop as emotions swept through him.

"Roger Twank-Tranquility," Charlie Duke stammered. "We copy you on the ground. You got a bunch of guys about to turn blue, we're breathing again. Thanks a lot."

Aldrin responded, a bit breathlessly, "Thank you!"

PROOF OF CONCEPT

Simply stated, NASA's extensive simulations had worked. The team's reaction to the computer alarms had been textbook. The SimSups had previously invented a nasty problem—a computer error with an obscure solution—and presented it to the controllers during a simulation. The trainees had choked on it, received a tongue-lashing, and then dug into the arcane alarm codes to work up a checklist and new rules. Had the simulation not included a flight computer error just over a week before landing, it is unlikely that anyone on the ground would have known what the hell it was, and they would probably have called an abort. Kranz would have had no choice but to accept, and the first moon landing attempt would have been a bust.

The ultimate test was the hair-raising landing. The computer was balky and they were flying long, too far downrange, and burning too much fuel over dangerously rocky territory. Armstrong had taken over control from the computer. The years of simulations, the hours of flying the dangerous LLRV, and time in the cockpits of fighter jets, the X-15, and Gemini spacecraft had all paid off. His intense concentration in a life-threatening situation came from hundreds of hours in artificial life-threatening situations (and a few grim minutes in very real ones) and had allowed him the laser focus required to bring *Eagle* down safely onto the Sea of Tranquility. Aldrin had stayed icy-cool and attended to the numbers—he later said that it was "just like the simulations." Likewise the ground controllers: their hundreds of hours of simulated flights had adapted out panic responses or rash action; they simply read the numbers, applied their prodigious intelligence to the problem, and helped the astronauts get down to the moon. But as for the actual flying, Armstrong and Aldrin were largely on their own.

And for Gene Kranz, former Marine pilot and longtime plank holder in Mission Control, it was all a matter of staying calm, observing the flight rules, keeping order, bringing out the best in his people, and, ultimately, learning when to let go.

At home, a few miles from Mission Control, Mrs. Kranz was already working on a new, even gaudier vest for *Apollo 12*.

INNOVATIONS:

- New and revolutionary training techniques born of World War II flight training, but exponentially more detailed and realistic.
- Defining problems discovered in these simulations and solving them, while developing new rules for the flight manual to be referred to quickly in an emergency.

:adowski, Calvin

Jnclaim : 2016-09-27

eld date : 2016-09-20
ickup location : Provincial Library

itle : Innovation the NASA way
harnessing the power of your organizatio
n for breakthrough success
Call number : 658.4063 PYLE
Item barcode : 39085900851870
Assigned branch : Regina - Central Adult B
ranch

Notification : Phone 1

Notes:

- Learning when to accept uncertainty and trust instinct.
- Adapting out fear, doubt, and hesitation in both ground personnel and pilot astronauts in real-time mission environments.
- For senior management, learning when to relinquish control to the person "in the cockpit."

CHAPTER 12

TOMORROWLAND: SAVING *SKYLAB*

CHALLENGES

- To choose a follow-on to the Apollo program that would maximize scientific return.
- To utilize the remaining moon program spacecraft in the most productive way possible.
- To rescue a space station that was damaged during launch.
- To assemble the best set of tools to do the job, in a kit that can fly in the Apollo capsule, in just a few days.
- Allow a crew of three to remain in orbit for up to two months.
- Allow for a wide range of experiments, primarily biomedical in nature.
- Create the first long-term life support apparatus.
- Conduct these operations on half of NASA's declining budget after Apollo.

WHAT'S NEXT?

As the Apollo program hit its stride in 1965, within NASA there was the obvious question: what's our next big act? If things went as planned, as many as 10 Apollo landers would soon take crews of two for increasingly ambitious stays on the moon's surface (in the end, six landings were completed). But the incredible flight hardware—and the remarkable human capital that had been forged at the various NASA centers—could not be allowed to go to waste once Apollo was completed. Layoffs were already starting as the Saturn V and Apollo spacecraft components were rolling off the assembly lines. Follow-on projects were needed, and the Apollo Applications Program office had been created to provide them.

The place itself was vanilla-plain, as were so many of NASA's program offices. It was in a nondescript room in a nondescript part of the Johnson Space Center. But appearances can be deceiving—this was ground zero for the lunar landing effort. The entire facility buzzed with the energy of a nation striving toward a common goal. But what would happen once that goal was reached was anyone's guess—the support that had been given so freely by Congress and the American public early on was already waning. So the tiny staff of the applications program spent their days dreaming up and studying post-Apollo missions utilizing the very capable orbiting outposts and lunar hardware. Trips to fly past Venus were analyzed, as were extended stays on the lunar surface.

And into the midst of this, a young Alan Bean, newly minted Apollo astronaut, was unceremoniously dumped. At 34, Bean was unremarkable looking: soft-faced, with a receding hairline but a ready smile. He was a sarsaparilla-sipping intellectual among the hard-drinking and pragmatic astronaut corps. Now he had been sent to Apollo Applications, which was viewed as a dead-end assignment in a space program that was all about the here-and-now of going to the moon. The AAP office flew exotic and cutting-edge missions on paper only. But as he always did, Bean decided to make the best of it. He would invest all the energy he had in this job.

His close friend and former test flight instructor in the Navy was Pete Conrad, 36. Conrad was in some ways the polar opposite of Bean. If you closed your eyes, he sounded like a space hero—wisecracking and arrogant, yet charismatic. But when you opened your eyes, you saw a 5' 8" bantam rooster with little hair and a yawning gap between his front teeth, which were often visible as he laughed at a joke coined at your expense. The guys loved him. He loved Al Bean. And he thought the Apollo Applications Program assignment was a raw deal. He called it "Tomorrowland," and not with admiration.

Of the many ideas papering the walls of the AAP office, perhaps the most promising was that of an Earth-orbiting space station. Since before the 1940s, people had been discussing the possibility of an orbital living complex. This discussion reached new heights when Wernher von Braun unveiled his plans for a huge military space station in the 1950s as a part of a unified program to reach out to the moon and Mars. But that was the stuff of fantasy, even now that the moon was within reach. Budgets and public sentiment would simply not support von Braun's massive program.

Al Bean was not obsessed with building a space station, either. Nor was he prone to daydream about what came after the moon landings. He just wanted a lunar flight so bad he could taste it. One afternoon, while he was laboring in the windowless offices, Conrad dropped in to see him. Al admired Pete—when Pete set his mind to getting something, like the commander's seat in *Apollo 12*, he got it. Al was the man who politely waited his turn. But today their fates would merge, because Pete had just dropped by to nonchalantly ask his friend Al Bean if he'd like to join him for the second moon landing. After a long, speechless moment, Al agreed, and he was soon off to training. While he was now living his dream of a lunar mission, he left AAP with a slight pang of guilt over work unfinished. What he did not know, nor could Pete Conrad, was that both their lives would soon be inextricably intertwined with one of the few AAP projects to make it off paper and into space. That project would be *Skylab*, and in 1973 it would fly into trouble.

CHALLENGE:

Conceptualize and design an affordable follow-on project to Apollo, utilizing surplus hardware.

THANKS FOR YOUR FINE WORK; HERE ARE YOUR PINK SLIPS

At NASA centers such as the Marshall Space Flight Center in Huntsville, which was overseen by Wernher von Braun himself, things were slowing down. While America had not yet landed on the moon, the bulk of the design work for Apollo was done. What remained was mostly overseeing the aerospace contractors as they built the hardware. Something new was needed to keep the brain trust together, and pink slips were arriving at many NASA field centers. Once these teams were gutted, they would not be easy to reassemble. They needed something new to work on.

Many schemes for orbiting stations had been researched over the years by contractors, the AAP office, and von Braun himself. As these were being considered, one from 1962 swam to the top of the stack: a McDonnell-Douglas proposal to build a station inside the Saturn's upper stage. It was more than big enough to make a splendid orbiting laboratory. This was the ultimate choice, and by the time the Apollo missions were heading off to the moon, a contract was signed with McDonnell-Douglas to build its S-IVB-based space station. It would be called *Skylab*.

SOLUTION:

Convert the existing third stage of the Saturn V rocket into a space station.

Now they needed to find a rocket to fly it on. The Saturn V assembly line would grind to a stop once the rocket for *Apollo 20* was completed. But the missions of *Apollos 18, 19,* and *20* were ultimately cancelled, and by 1970 there were spare Saturn V's aplenty. *Skylab* had its ride.

CHALLENGE:

Make a space station, essentially a big "tin can," livable while observing weight and avoiding flammable materials.

As final touches were put on the hardware to convert the fuel tank into a station, some thought was given to what it would be like to live inside it for extended periods of time. NASA was a minimalist organization, and until now, space capsules had been small and had never been used for more than two weeks. There was not much room for interior design in a capsule, and it would have been eschewed by the Spartan astronaut corps at any rate. But a space station was different; it was a place where people would actually live and work. NASA ultimately realized that having crews of three living inside a gray, featureless "can" for up to three months might create some stress.

The agency reached out to the famed industrial designer Raymond Loewy. Loewy had designed, among other things, the Studebaker Avanti sportscar, a streamlined steam locomotive, and the Greyhound Scenicruiser bus. He seemed a reasonable choice to design an orbiting environment that would assure the mental well-being of America's heroes, the *Apollo/Skylab* astronauts. His contributions included the interior color scheme, a wardroom where the astronauts could eat and relax, and the placement of a large window from which to admire the Earth below. The window became the favorite gathering place of the *Skylab* crews and contributed greatly to their endurance.

SOLUTION:

Hire the finest and most daring industrial designer of the era—an unusual move for a conservative, pragmatic agency like NASA— to design your space station's interior.

LAUNCH DAY BLUES

On May 14, 1973, *Skylab 1* was launched on the final Saturn V to fly into space. The remaining moon rockets would be trundled off to the various space centers to be put on display, the most expensive museum exhibits in history at about $500 million apiece.

CHALLENGE:

Identify damage to your ailing space station, then plan a rescue mission, with limited situational awareness.

The launch *looked* perfect and inserted *Skylab* into orbit. But all was not well with NASA's first space station. Within the hour, Houston began to get odd readings back from *Skylab*. Mission Control hoped at first that what they were seeing came from a bad sensor or inaccurate readouts on the ground. But all too soon the truth became evident: *Skylab* was in trouble, and it was bad. The amount of power from the solar panels was way too low—perhaps 20 percent of what was needed to properly run the station—and temperatures were soaring inside, rapidly heading to 120, then 130 degrees Fahrenheit (°F). The combination of these two phenomena would wreck *Skylab* within a few weeks if they were not addressed.

But before they could fix it, the astronauts needed to know what had gone wrong. With a lot of detective work, aided by some long-range photos from an Air Force satellite passing nearby, they had their culprit. *Skylab* had two folding solar panels that sat flush along its sides during launch. Also along the side of the fusilage was a large sheet-metal micrometeoroid and heat shield. Once in orbit, the twin solar panels were supposed to spread like wings and lock perpendicular to the station, and the micrometeoroid shield would shade the hull . That was the plan.

During launch, however, once the rocket had gone supersonic about 50 seconds into the flight, some of that fast-moving air had found its way under the leading edge of the micrometeoroid shield. It ripped free and fluttered down into the Atlantic below. One of the solar panels came unlatched at the same time and broke free from *Skylab* shortly after reaching orbit. To make matters worse, the second solar panel on the other side was damaged as well, though it was still attached.

Once *Skylab* was in orbit, four smaller solar panels unfurled from the forward end as planned. But when they tried to unfold the two main solar panels, which provided the vast majority of the power, the starboard side was stuck fast and the other side appeared to be *gone*. There was barely enough power to run basic functions.

SOLUTION:

Use a combination of ground-based cameras, orbiting military satellites, and inferences from technical data to diagnose problems.

Then there was the missing micrometeoroid and heat shield. Its main purpose besides protecting *Skylab* from little meteoroids was to shade the station's hull from the blistering effects of direct exposure to sunlight in space. Without it, the hull paint would blister and temperatures inside the station would soar. Eventually the interior and instrumentation would be destroyed and the structure itself could be compromised.

Pete Conrad had been scheduled to depart the next day with his crew of two other astronauts in a surplus Apollo capsule to rendezvous with *Skylab*. A part of him had wanted Al Bean to fly with him, just as on *Apollo 12*, but Bean instead got command of the next *Skylab* mission, and that made both men happy. But generous of heart as Conrad was, right about now he could not be blamed if he wanted to change places with Bean. Conrad's departure would be delayed until they could figure out how to fix *Skylab*, if it could be fixed at all. Failure to do this would cancel his mission and Bean's as well, and Conrad was not about to let that happen. He was instantly ready to convert his commissioning flight into a salvage effort.

CHALLENGE:

Quickly invent robust and flexible repair techniques for barely understood problems.

QUICK FIXES

In a frenzied collaboration of a sort not seen since the *Apollo 13* emergency, NASA engineers came together with the contractors who had built *Skylab* in an effort to find a solution, and quickly. This was innovation by emergency, a time when NASA and its suppliers were often at their best. The answers needed to be found in hours and days, not weeks.

There were two major problems. The first was the overheating issue—they needed to protect the station from direct sunlight via some kind of curtain or shade. The second problem was the stuck solar panel on the side. With the port-side panel gone, it was critical to fully extend the starboard-side panel. Without knowing exactly what was wrong, they went about designing solutions. It must be remembered that whatever procedures were eventually chosen needed to be (1) easy to operate and deploy, (2) lightweight, (3) robust enough to last for at least 90 days, and preferably a year, (4) safe to fly up with, and (5) able to fit in the already cramped confines of the Apollo capsule, while leaving the three crew members room to move about. Talk about shooting in the dark.

And time was of the essence. The sun was baking the station to Death Valley temperatures. Food was spoiling, and interior plastics were deforming and could melt. Wire insulation could be compromised. And possibly most dangerous was an invisible killer: there were chemicals that could outgas when the interior plastics were heated that were highly toxic and could scuttle the mission. So they had to deal with the heating issues first.

Many proposals came forward from both the contractors and NASA personnel. Cloth shades, inflatable structures, even spray paint and commercial wallpaper were seriously considered to protect the slowly blistering hull. But it was NASA's Huntsville and Houston centers that came up with the ultimate solution.

SOLUTION:

Work closely with contractors and NASA engineers to come up with procedures that might work. Test these solutions with simulations.

The engineers at the Johnson Space Center devised the quickest fix: a large nylon parasol that could be shoved up through a nearby airlock and deployed much like a huge beach umbrella. A JSC technician was sent into town to buy some fishing poles from a local sporting goods shop, along with the strongest nylon line he could find. The fabric came from a parachute found at JSC. The engineers jury-rigged the contraption and tested it inside an empty workshop, then hastily arranged a demonstration for the NASA brass. Eyebrows shot up and doubting faces looked on as what amounted to a gigantic beach umbrella was unfolded, but in the end it got a thumbs-up from the managers and, just as important, the *Skylab* crew.

The Marshall Space Flight Center in Hunstsville, not to be outdone, came up with a nylon curtain that would fold up like a window shade. There were two 50-foot fiberglass poles to hold one end and push out the other. The shade covered a larger area, but it had to be deployed either from the capsule or from an open airlock. This would require a true extravehicular activity (EVA), and NASA had not had much luck with detailed work in EVAs. But it was the only way they could think of to cover the broader expanse that would remain after the parasol did its limited work.

Then there was that second problem: the stuck solar panel. When the heat shield tore off during ascent, part of it got wrapped around the remaining solar panel. It was like aluminum roofing material—thin, sharp, and clingy. Worse yet, rivets had been used in its construction, and a few of them had now embedded themselves into the solar panel. It was *really* stuck, and undoing it would take a major effort.

CHALLENGE:

Develop, in record time, compact and safe tools to repair the stricken spacecraft.

For this challenge, the engineers sourced a commercial tree-pruning pole and a clipper head designed for cutting power cables. In an age of intense specialization and multimillion-dollar lunar rock hammers, this off-the-shelf tool was a very low-tech solution that seemed out of keeping with the NASA way of doing things. But that was also the charm of it: this was a case of "just get it done" and to hell with the studies and formal risk assessments (there was no time). There was a risk in taking these relatively untried tools into space inside the Apollo capsule, but the NASA of 1973 was far less risk-averse than it is today, and it was deemed an acceptable compromise. The cable-snipper would be used to cut the metal restraining the solar panel, then an attached rope could be utililized to pull it into place.

SOLUTION:

Wherever possible, use off-the-shelf components and existing low-tech solutions. *Keep it simple.* Test tools on the ground and make them modular so that they can fit inside the cramped Apollo capsule.

The shade contraptions and cable-snipper were extensively tested by fellow astronaut Rusty Schweickart in the Marshall water tank. When he explained how it would work to Conrad and his crew, they laughed. It looked like something Wile E. Coyote would fabricate to trap the Road Runner, but they were willing to give it a shot.

Conrad's crewmate Joe Kerwin then joined Schweickart in the water and practiced extensively in the tank, learning as much as was possible in the simulated environment with the limited time left.

While these may not have been the most elegant or well-worked-out solutions, they were far simpler and cheaper than what we would see today, and developed in record time. NASA had already lost one launch window for the repair (they occurred every five or six days), and had to make the next one to be in time to save the station. It was a frenzied week. There were a few nervous breakdowns and more than one technician got in trouble for overdedication. In one case, an engineer worked so late that the gates outside Johnson had been locked for the night. Having not seen home for many days, he lost his patience and climbed the fence, roughly twice his height, barbed wire and all. The result was a deep cut in his buttocks and, after he fell on the other side, a thorough chewing out by a security team. But NASA's people got the *Skylab* fixes ready with time to spare.

Meanwhile, patience was evaporating as quickly as the sun-blasted paint on *Skylab*. Pete Conrad's statement was typical of his test pilot brethren. "Just get me *up there*, goddamn it!" He knew that if a way could be found to fix the thing, his crew could do it. But he needed to get there.

PETE CONRAD TO THE RESCUE

On May 25, 11 frantic days after the troubled launch of *Skylab*, Conrad, Weitz, and Kerwin were strapped inside their Apollo Command Module. *Skylab*'s roadside service call was about to commence. A flash of flame and Conrad, Weitz, and Kerwin were off to rescue their space station.

In typical Conrad-ese, the veteran astronaut yelled "Skylab tally-ho!" as he closed in on the stricken space station. But upon closer inspection, he was more subdued. The station was a real mess (this was the first confirmation of the extent of the damage), and their repairs would be touch-and-go. But they had to try.

Conrad pulled the Command Module abreast of *Skylab*. With his crew suited up and ready to go, they depressurized and opened the hatch. Weitz assembled the cable-cutter and, with Kerwin holding him by the ankles, floated out of the capsule in an attempt to wrest the pinned solar panel remains free. They could now see close up how the twisted heat shield had gotten pulled around a section of the remaining solar panel, holding it fast. It was a mess. The harder Weitz pulled and tugged on the cable-cutter, the closer the capsule got to smashing into the station. Conrad had to fire the thrusters furiously to avoid a dangerous impact. This used much of their maneuvering fuel and left Conrad feeling queasy. He later remarked that it made him nervous as hell, nearly banging many millions of dollars worth of Apollo moonship against many millions worth of *Skylab*.

CHALLENGE:

Repair procedures do not work as intended.

After a 22-hour day it was time to dock and catch some sleep. They tried to dock with *Skylab*, but that wouldn't work either. This was simply not their day. Conrad tried and tried, giving it a bit more thrust each time. Finally, they put their pressure suits back on, depressurized again, and, as Conrad nudged the Command Module's docking capsule against the docking collar on *Skylab*, Kerwin crawled into the tunnel, removed the front hatch, and snipped a couple of wires in the docking rig. This had the effect of overriding some of the safety protocols—like they cared about *that* anymore—and the docking latches slammed shut, locking the craft together. They all hoped that the latches would let go when the time came to go home.

Their first task was to sample the air inside *Skylab* for toxins. They took out their hastily contrived test kits, went into the airlock, and sampled some *Skylab* air from a vent tube. All was well. They entered visors up, only to be greeted with 130 degrees of stale air. So off came the spacesuits and the crew entered America's first space station in their underwear.

Once inside, they were able to deploy the jury-rigged parasol through an airlock. The thing actually worked, and the temperatures inside started to drop. The trio started to activate the station, although food and water were consumed cold and very few lights and circuits were turned on, as they were still experiencing a massive power deficit. That—the second problem—would have to be dealt with, and soon.

On day 14, they prepared for the EVA to fix the solar panel. Everyone knew that NASA had not enjoyed much luck with EVAs. Even though it had flown a number of successful moon landings now, the last real experience with actually working weightless in space was during Gemini. Only on the final flight of that series had Buzz Aldrin finally shown that it could be done safely and effectively. Now, with those lessons in mind and a lot of underwater simulation, they were going to play for much higher stakes. The future of their mission, and the two to follow, depended on their success.

Houston sent up revised and updated instructions for the procedure (everything at NASA has a *procedure*) to *Skylab*'s teleprinter. The printout was almost 15 feet long. How much attention Conrad paid to it is not recorded, nor are his words when he saw it. But knowing the man's history, they were likely to be salty.

Conrad and Kerwin left the toasty interior of *Skylab* the next day to begin work on the snagged solar panel while Weitz remained behind where he could observe their progress through a window. The two emerged from the airlock with a bushel each of equipment—fiberglass poles, rope, the cutting head, and miscellaneous odds and ends. They looked like a space-suited municipal tree maintenance crew.

The general idea was for Kerwin to first mount the cutter onto about 25 feet of fiberglass pole. Since the outside of *Skylab* was smooth and mostly devoid of handholds or grips, they would hook the cutter onto the offending metal shroud with the long pole, Conrad would then hand-over-hand himself over to the end of the solar panel, tie off a piece of rope, come back, and affix the other end of the rope to whatever was handy. Then he and Kerwin would tug on the rope to cut through the mangled heat shield, it would spring free, and the solar panel would swing into its open position and lock. Life would be good, the two men would reenter *Skylab*, and lions and lambs would lie down together worldwide. That was the plan.

Down in Houston, Mission Control was fretting. They had discussed the procedure at length, and many of them had been concerned about the "what-ifs." What if the metal shield remains could not be cut? What if it tore free, ricocheted, and cut open one of the astronauts' suits? What if a rope snapped and whiplashed, somehow tangling with an astronaut and dooming him? What if something else broke free and somehow smacked one of the spacewalkers, disabling him and forcing his companion (possibly also injured) to leave him outside? What if, what if?

SOLUTION:

Adapt to the situation, taking some calculated risks in a totally unforgiving environment. Invent procedures as you see fit on-site.

Clearly they did not know Pete Conrad well enough, because if they had, they would have known that neither nature, *Skylab*, nor the good Lord would dare to get in his way. But Conrad knew it, and that was what mattered.

Kerwin set about trying to slip the cutting jaws over the heat shield, but he could not brace himself and 25 feet of whipping pole enough to get purchase. Conrad was nonplussed. Then one of them noticed a small D-ring protruding from the side of *Skylab*—neither of them knew why it was there, and neither cared. All they knew was that they could tie some rope to that to steady Kerwin, and they did.

In short order he had the jaws of the cutter firmly clenched around the metal shield.

Now it was Conrad's turn. While Kerwin caught his breath, Conrad slithered along the pole and worked his way out to the end of the solar panel trailing a length of rope. He tied it off and worked his way back toward Kerwin, only to have the cutter jaws pick that moment to jerk and cut the restraining metal free. The panel swung out about 20 degrees, and the pole drifted away—as did Conrad, "ass over teakettle" as he described it. He reeled himself back with his tether, and the two men surveyed their handiwork. The heat shield was clear, but now a damping strut was preventing the panel from opening out the full 90 degrees. It too needed to go. Why was nothing ever as simple as in the simulations?

A TIME FOR DARING—AND LAUGHTER

With the rope now tied off at both ends—one on the far side of the solar panel and the other near the hatch—they tightened it. Then, after Conrad briefed Kerwin on an unorthodox and totally ad-hoc procedure, both men climbed underneath the taut rope and caught their breath. On the count of three, they grunted and stood up together like two Olympic weight lifters. The errant damper snapped, the solar panel swung free, and once again the astronauts cartwheeled into space.

Laughing and huffing, dangling from their tethers, they hauled themselves back to *Skylab* for the last time. Their work was done. Between breaths, Conrad described the rest of their procedure to panicked controllers on the ground after the fact—nobody had been entirely clear on what he had planned. The two inventive astronauts returned to the airlock and went inside while blood pressures on the ground retreated. Then, Mission Control was treated to another stream of salty language as Conrad narrated the experience to Weitz, laughing all the while.

Temperatures stabilized, the power flow increased dramatically, and *Skylab* was now sufficiently stabilized for the remainder of their 28-day mission. Ingenuity and NASA know-how—along with no small amount of daring on the part of the astronauts—had come to the rescue of a badly crippled spacecraft. The crew would spend the remainder of the mission completing repairs, conducting science experiments, and exploring exercise regimens for zero-g conditioning.

CHALLENGE:

Keeping mentally calm and focused during challenging—and dangerous—situations in space.

The fix was effective but unorthodox. The "procedure" had been risky, and Conrad's on-the-spot command decisions had made it even more so. But they had persevered, had overcome daunting odds, and had saved the mission. In the process of doing so, they had nearly given Mission Control a collective heart attack, and Conrad would not have had it any other way. For his efforts, he received the Congressional Space Medal of Honor. In subsequent years, despite being the third man to walk on the moon, he would always count *Skylab* as his favorite mission.

SOLUTION:

When possible, train and simulate, including all likely variables. Then lead with confidence, boldness, and positivity (and even humor).

Two other crews would follow, the next commanded by Pete's old pal Al Bean. He would complete the repairs to *Skylab* and double Conrad's endurance record. In hindsight, it seemed that Apollo

Applications was not Tomorrowland after all . . . it was Adventureland. And *Skylab* was their Magic Kingdom.

INNOVATIONS

- Created a sophisticated space station from surplus Apollo-program components.
- Designed a series of astrophysical and biomedical experiments for a weightless environment.
- Created a successful long-duration life support system.
- Responded to launch damage in record time, designing tools and procedures within 10 days.
- Flew a successful rescue mission to repair the damaged station.
- Crew improvised repair procedures when plans did not pan out.
- Flew three crews to a compromised station, including one stay of 84 days.
- Gained data that were useful to later NASA operations, including the International Space Station of the 1990s/2000s.

CHAPTER 13

PROJECT VIKING: LOOKING FOR LIFE ON MARS

CHALLENGES

- To design and build a robotic spacecraft that can fly to Mars, then send landers to its surface.
- In an age when computers filled whole rooms, to create one that can pilot and navigate that lander and function for years in a hostile environment, yet is small enough to fly.
- To design and build a life science laboratory, also normally the size of a small room, that can fit onto a Mars lander.
- To define a series of portable experiments to discover microbes on Mars, if they exist.
- To push past academic and scientific resistance to new ideas about detecting such life on another world.
- Over time, to reinterpret these results as newer techniques and more Mars data are available.

LOOKING FOR LIFE

In 1976, *Viking 1* landed on Mars. This was an innovative first on a number of levels: the first spacecraft to successfully land and complete its mission on another planet, the first images returned from the surface of Mars, and many others. But perhaps most remarkable, it was also the first time that any machine (or person, for that matter) would undertake the search for life on another world.

This part of the mission presented, as you might expect, an enormous challenge. First off, there was a large contingent of scientists, engineers, and politicians who felt that Viking's goals were overreaching—that landing the first spacecraft on another planet and taking pictures, measuring weather, and examining the soil was plenty to undertake. In a way, they were right; that would have been challenging enough. Landing on Mars is still hard today, and to reach for these goals in the 1960s was audacious. But still more ambitious were the life-seeking experiments added to Viking. This single requirement would soon devour more resources, and cause more controversy, than any other part of the mission.

Talk about innovation: this part of the Viking program would have to be created from whole cloth. While the Jet Propulsion Laboratory (JPL) had been flying to Mars and the rest of the solar system since the early 1960s, nothing even remotely like this had been tried before. Not even the Soviets, who tended to be ahead of the curve in robotic exploration daring (although not engineering), had tried anything this ambitious. It was a leap into the unknown, and the space age was only a few years old when the planning for this began. Computers like the IBM System/360 filled entire rooms, and there was simply no model to follow for a small life-science lab, much less one that would survive the torturous flight to Mars, the tumultuous landing, and the savage surface conditions. The temperature swings on Mars could range from a comparatively balmy 70 degrees Fahrenheit (°F) to almost 200 below, and dust storms routinely ravaged the surface. But this did not stop the Viking planning team.

A small team of biology professors and life-science researchers went about the arduous task of figuring out a way to test for life on

Mars, even though they had absolutely no idea what such life might look like. This was 1965, when *Mariner 4* had just returned the first data from Mars. Critical decisions had to be made on the scanty data, and a framework of assumptions had to be agreed upon.

CHALLENGE:

Design a science investigation protocol for the first machines to land on Mars.

- **Assumptions 1**
  1. Mars has an atmosphere that is composed largely of carbon dioxide, potentially friendly to plants and possibly microorganisms.
  2. Mars is very dry.
  3. Liquid water does not exist on Mars today.
  4. The atmospheric pressure is *very* low, and temperatures are extreme.

As Israel Taback, a deputy project manager for Viking, wryly stated:

> *We took a really long chance and we started with life experiments, instead of looking for water first, which we knew about. But we did look for life instead.*

This approach may have been premature—virtually nothing was known about possible organisms on Mars. It would be decades before extremophiles—organisms found on Earth that exist in traditionally toxic and deadly conditions, such as those found in the Antarctic dry valleys and deep, hot ocean vents—were even discovered. But this very lack of knowledge in 1965 serves to underscore the daring nature of the Viking experiments.

But what exactly should they search for? Another set of assumptions was needed.

SOLUTION:

Distribute the research across disciplines—chemistry, geology, seismology, and meteorology (among others)—but concentrate the majority of the lander's capability on life science.

- **Assumptions 2**
    1. Life on Mars will be carbon-based (like on Earth).
    2. Life on Mars will probably be microbial or tiny plants.
    3. Life on Mars will metabolize nutrients in a way similar to Earth-based life, and the same basic nutrients will work.

CANALS AND MARTIANS

All this said, there was still a romanticized belief in some quarters (even among some scientists) that a variant of Percival Lowell's Mars could still exist in one form or another. Though most doubted that artificially created canals crisscrossed the surface or that intelligent life was using telescopes to observe Earth at that very minute, many felt that plants might cover a significant portion of the planet and that the atmosphere might not be as hostile as the skeptics believed. Romance dies hard, or, as one of the scientist-leaders of the life-science experiments, Dr. Norman Horowitz, put it:

> *It's hard to convey in a few words the total commitment people had in those days [the early 1960s] to an Earth-like Mars.*

> *This was an inheritance from Percival Lowell. It's amazing: in pre-Sputnik 1 days, in fact, up till 1963, well into the space age, people were still confirming results that Lowell had obtained [though his telescope]; totally erroneous results. It [was] simply bizarre!*

CHALLENGE:

Design science experiments to find life on Mars and make them small enough to fly there.

In other words, in Horowitz's view, tradition and romanticism were the enemies of innovation. To innovate, in his argument, would be to toss out the nineteenth-century vision of Mars as Earthlike and treat this first landing mission as a flight to a dead, desert world. And in the post-*Mariner 4* era and in which they were entering, that was a solid call. In Horowitz's view, the general design that was being put forward, based on the idea that any Martian organisms would behave like Earthly ones, was deeply flawed. If something existed there, which he frankly doubted, it would not be familiar to us, and it might well not be detected using traditional methods.

SOLUTION:

1. Created a model that characterized what life on Mars might be like.
2. Designed ingenious, highly miniaturized experiments to fly there and investigate.

On the same science team was Dr. Gilbert Levin, who was in many wa opposite of Horowitz. He was in some respects one of the "romanticists" that Horowitz spoke of, although he would not have referred to himself in that way, and he certainly did not believe in canals or intelligent Martians. Levin wanted to use a simple set of experiments on the Viking lander to determine the presence (or lack) of microbial life using added nutrients that would nourish Earthly—and possibly Martian—organisms.

Levin's experiment was called Labeled Release, and it would gather a soil sample and deposit it into a container. This bit of dirt would have some liquid nutrients added, which was often characterized as a sort of "chicken-broth" solution. This would be allowed to sit for a time, allowing any microorganisms to metabolize the nutrients. There was also carbon 14, a traceable isotope of regular carbon, in the broth. When the air in the container, a bit of Martian atmosphere trapped within, was later released, it would be monitored for any trace of gases that might contain the 14C (remember that it was only in the broth, not in the air); if that carbon isotope was found, it might indicate that some kind of organism had "eaten" the broth (and the 14C) and then, in effect, exhaled the 14C.

Horowitz's instrument was similar but more limited in scope. Called the Pyrolitic Release Experiment, it would also start with a scoop of Martian soil and dump it into an onboard container, but after that, the assumptions diverged. In Horowitz's design, the soil was left to soak in gases that also included carbon 14. After a few days, the soil sample would he heated to high temperatures to incinerate any organisms in the soil. Analytical instruments would capture any gases leaving as a result of the "burn," and if 14C was released, it *might* be an indication of carbon fixation, one way in which microorganisms make their living. If there was a positive result, the sample would be heated again; if the same thing happened twice, it would probably indicate some kind of nonlife chemical reaction. If it happened only the first time, it was probably the result of burnt-up critters.

Two other experiments were included in Viking's life-science package. One was called the Gas Chromatograph–Mass Spectrometer (GCMS), which monitored yet another soil sample, this one untreated in any way, for traces of organic compounds (living or not) when the soil was heated. The final experiment was called Gas Exchange. It too used a small sample of Martian soil, added the nutrient broth, replaced the Martian air in the container with helium, and then heated it. It then measured any gases released, again working on the assumption that organisms would "eat" the broth and give off metabolism-created gases.

The primary difference in approaches was a bright line between Horowitz's approach and Levin's. In Horowitz's experiment, no nutrients were added, and any organisms that were in the soil would do what they would do, unassisted. In Levin's approach, the Labeled Release and Gas Exchange experiments, a broad assumption was made that any Martian organisms would eat, then metabolize, the added nutrient broth just like Earthly ones did. The results of that would be measured.

In the new science of exobiology, this seemingly small difference was a world apart from Horowitz's. And on such differences major battle lines are often drawn. In this case, this difference in approaches would cause acrimony between members of the two teams for well over 30 years.

LAB-IN-A-BOX

All these instruments, each cutting-edge for the 1970s, had to be crammed into a box smaller than three feet on each axis and weighing less than 35 pounds. And in a spacecraft that had to leave Earth, cruise to Mars, and land there, each ounce was critical.

Teams of engineers and designers joined forces to bring the needed hardware down to the required size and weight parameters. It was a daunting task; these were traditionally large, heavy laboratory instruments, and making them small, light, and robust enough to fly to Mars was a huge challenge, but in the end it was done, and with great elegance. It was all cutting-edge design, and the cost reflected this: a billion dollars. This was a big number in 1976 money; it would be closer to six billion today. To use a term later associated with NASA's space program, failure was not an option.

WHERE TO LAND?

Both Viking spacecraft flew to Mars uneventfully, entering orbit around the planet in June of 1976. The orbiters snapped photos of Mars—the first close-ups to be taken since *Mariner 9* in 1971— and mission planners looked at the new images in horror.

CHALLENGE:

Find a landing site on a planet that had previously been mapped only in very low resolution.

The *Mariner 9* images had enjoyed, at best, an image resolution of about 300 feet *per pixel.* Anything smaller than that was essentially invisible—a World War II destroyer would barely be seen. If you wanted to know more about an area, you had to infer by looking at the broader, general topography. It was an inexact science.

Then the pictures from the Viking orbiters came back, and what a surprise they were. The close-up shots could discern objects as small as 26 feet . . . and what terrors appeared at this scale! Selected landing areas that had been thought to be flat and relatively clear of dangerous obstructions were now seen to be rocky minefields. And bear in mind that anything much bigger than a basketball could seriously inhibit or even damage the lander, so you can imagine the tension over landing site selection. It was still a process of inference and guesswork.

SOLUTION:

Obtain higher-resolution imagery rapidly from Viking's own orbiters, then evaluate the terrain based on (1) overall similarities to Earth, (2) the topography of sites on Mars, and (3) intuition.

The new images were studied in agonizing detail. Old landing site arguments were torn open and bled once again. Previously rejected areas were reconsidered. But in the end, they moved only a short distance from their original site selection. Two areas selected from a roughly equatorial band had been chosen from the *Mariner 9* photos; the landing zones were merely adjusted to reflect new knowledge about the terrain. *Viking 1* would land on Chryse Planitia and *Viking 2* on the far side of Mars in Utopia Planitia.

This settled, commands were sent to Mars, and the landers separated from the orbiters, descending to opposite sides of the planet. The orbiters continued circling overhead. Once on Mars, each lander gathered soil samples and dumped them into the experiment package to seek results. And here is where the divergence between the approaches to the question of finding life—both of them innovative and clever, but based on different assumptions—got ugly.

LIFE! OR PERHAPS NOT . . .

To greatly simplify, the experiments based on Horowitz's assumptions, and his Gas Exchange experiment, returned negligible results, as he suspected they would. Anything found could be attributed to either nonorganic (and thus nonlife) reactions and/or instrument background noise.

The GCMS instrument registered a flat zero result, largely confirming Horowitz's results.

However, Levin's Labeled Release experiment showed a greater than expected result, and quickly. A jolt of excitement ran through the researchers. However, it also declined quickly—too quickly—and the results, when measured over time, did not add up. Something was screwy.

In the end, most of those involved agreed that the results of Levin's experiment were probably a false positive and that some chemical in the Martian soil was reacting to the liquid injected into the sample, mimicking life. It was hypothesized that an oxidizing agent, possibly perchlorate (similar to the hydrogen peroxide used in hair-bleaching chemicals on Earth) was causing the sample to react the way it did.

But Levin did not back down. He remained convinced that they had probably found something living. A decade later, he and Horowitz nearly came to blows outside a scientific symposium on the subject, so strong were their feelings. Insults flew, and nothing was resolved. The complexity of their endeavor, and of operating such complicated instruments from millions of miles away, assured that neither of their arguments had come any closer to resolution in the intervening 10 years.

VIKING'S ENCORE

CHALLENGE:

How to interpret 30-year-old data with new knowledge.

In a final coda, early in the twenty-first century, a scientist named Dr. Chris McKay thought that Viking's results might be worth a new look. Working at NASA's Ames Research Center, McKay worked with soil samples taken from one of the most arid and sterile environments on Earth: the perchlorate-infused Atacama desert in

Peru. He subjected these samples to some of the same experiments that Viking had used on Mars. This time, however, he took the presence of perchlorate in the soil into account when interpreting the results. A subsequent mission, the *Mars Phoenix Lander*, which reached the planet in 2008, had confirmed the presence of the chemical in Martian soil near the north pole. Armed with this, when McKay completed his experiments, he found that soil with organic compounds (in this case, microorganisms) gave generally the same result that Levin's instrument had. What was new was that McKay now understood that the perchlorate destroyed organic molecules when heated. The debate was reopened and smolders to this day. But for McKay, it's no longer an open question: "Contrary to 30 years of perceived wisdom, Viking did detect organic materials on Mars." That's his conclusion. It's a strong statement coming from the disciplined mind of a scientist.

SOLUTION:

Repeat the experiment here on Earth, using the most Marslike sample available and new data from other Mars landers.

The Viking landers conducted atmospheric tests, gathered meteorological data, measured "Marsquakes," and studied soil dynamics for years. The orbiters wheeled silently overhead, taking millions of pictures and relaying them home to Earth. The vast library of data from both sets of spacecraft is being studied to this day. But it was the life-science experiments—that possibly naïve search for Earth-like microbes—that so stirred the popular imagination. It would seem that the average person is far more interested in finding *things* on Mars—living things—than in knowing mere facts, and this is understandable. But the Viking mission, robust as it was, left this question wide open.

Such is the price of innovation. Without the brilliant work of teams of dedicated engineers and scientists, the Viking experiments could have waited at least 20 more years to fly. And even then, the results might have been a mixed bag. As it is, the question of life on Mars remains. The current Mars rover *Curiosity* has found hints of organic carbon, but this proves only that organic compounds may exist on Mars; it is not equipped to directly discern living things (organic compounds can come from meteors or other nonliving sources). Any certain answer must await a new, more sophisticated rover or a return of Martian soil to Earth, a mission that is now under consideration.

Sometimes great innovation causes equal amounts of pain and reward, and such was the case with Viking. But it was a stirring start, a daring bit of Earthly hubris in an age where such things seemed possible. We assumed life to be as simple as we found it on Earth's surface and went about finding it on Mars in that way. Then, in the intervening decades, we discovered much more about life on our own planet (and in its oceans, deserts, and poles) that reset our assumptions. We now apply this new understanding to future Mars missions, which will follow up on the flawed but noble work begun by Viking: the search for living things on Mars.

INNOVATIONS

- Blended the best of government, industry, and academia to accomplish a robotic mission that was decades ahead of its time.
- Managed highly divergent science disciplines—and egos—in a collaborative work environment.
- Shrank the needed instrumentation from the size of a laboratory to the size of a microwave oven.

- Launched, navigated, and landed—across more than a hundred million miles of space—a large robotic probe on Mars at a time when four-function hand-held calculators were just coming into fashion.
- Performed life science experiments on Mars and generated results, albeit confusing ones.
- Decades later, based on new data from Mars and new understanding of the nature of life and soil chemistry on Earth, reinterpreted Viking data to conclude that it probably did find organic substances—and possibly life—on Mars.

CHAPTER 14

INTO THE GREAT DARKNESS: VOYAGER'S INCREDIBLE JOURNEY

CHALLENGES

- Design and operate the first semiautonomous computer ever used in space exploration.
- Create a spacecraft capable of surviving at least a decade in the cold, high-radiation environments of the outer planets.
- Design a navigation system capable of keeping the twin spacecraft on course for billions of miles.
- Obtain continued funding for a science program that could last almost 50 years.
- While observing cultural and political considerations, design an information recording to be housed within the spacecraft with a message from Earth that could be interpreted by alien life forms.
- Maintain a technical proficiency, in both hardware and software management, for spacecraft technology that will be increasingly out of date.

A WILD RIDE, A CONFUSED COMPUTER

August 1977. It was quiet inside the rocket's payload shroud, about 160 feet above the hissing, vapor-enshrouded launchpad below. The only sounds were the muted hiss of cryogenic fuels topping off the top stage, immediately below, and the whirring of the gyros inside *Voyager 2*. And then, all hell broke loose.

There was a roar, then a thud as the solid boosters ignited and the explosive bolts holding the Titan rocket released the straining machine from the launchpad. It rose slowly at first, then picked up speed rapidly. The Titan itself gave a pretty smooth ride, but the solid boosters—which would burn for only a couple of minutes—shook the spacecraft like an industrial vibrator. It was a slam-bang ride.

Then the solids burned out and fell away, and the Titan's remaining liquid-fueled engines hummed along like a big electric motor. The rocket had rolled over onto its back to follow the most efficient path to an equatorial orbit, and it was following this course as set by the booster's flight computers. It continued on its journey to fling *Voyager 2* into interplanetary space.

But all was not well up inside the nose cone. While the Titan's upper stage continued the journey, *Voyager 2* was quietly experiencing its own version of digital panic. The computer had been designed to be semiautonomous for the long trip to Jupiter and beyond. Its designers had programmed it to deal with whatever contingencies they could imagine once it was in space. But in the first few minutes of that trip, the rocket had been programmed to roll over onto its back as it left Earth—standard procedure—and *Voyager* had not been informed of this. Its onboard computer was not happy, and started trying to isolate and bypass what it thought must be a faulty component.

CHALLENGE:

Build an autonomous computer with 1970s technology that can power a spacecraft to the edge of the solar system.

Luckily, the Titan had its own guidance system, so *Voyager's* computer was not affecting the flight path with its brief panic. It did, however, assume that something must be wrong, possibly with its own senses. The computer switched to the backup system, but the news was the same. It knew that it was twisting into space, and that was not supposed to happen. It was a cybernetic version of vertigo.

Just over an hour into the flight, things had quieted down a bit. A smaller solid rocket fired to give the spacecraft its final push away from Earth. As planned, the event timer (its internal clock) unfolded two long booms from the central structure of the craft—one with the nuclear fuel source, the other with a sensor array. But even though the computer had triggered this event, a part of it "felt" the twin shocks of the booms unfurling and reacted by firing the probe's small thrusters—those intended to correct its attitude in space—to compensate. Then the "cerebral cortex" of the computer (the executive program) challenged *that* action. It was like a brain experiencing being bipolar and schizophrenic all at once. Finally, in desperation, the spacecraft exercised its final option: it stopped talking to Earth altogether.

The intended purpose of this procedure was in case of an emergency in deep space. If the probe somehow lost contact with Earth, it was to cease communication and begin a search protocol, scanning for an incoming signal from the controllers on the ground. The tiny ship began a logical and ordered sweep to find the sun and the Earth. The sad fact was that it had never really lost contact in the first place—it just thought it had.

After nearly 80 minutes of this, it finally found what it was looking for and settled down—for the moment.

On the ground, Jet Propulsion Laboratory (JPL) engineers and programmers breathed a huge sigh of relief, then swung into emergency mode. Among them was John Casani, who had been living and breathing Voyager for more than two years as the project manager. Tall and laconic, the fiftyish Casani knew that he had a problem out in space, and that he and his team had to find a way to fix it. Their autonomous spacecraft had turned out to be tantrum-prone.

Specifically, when the Titan had rolled over on its back to achieve the proper heading into orbit, the guidance gyros inside *Voyager*, which were designed to sense gradual changes, had slammed against their stops. When the computer sensed that a guidance gyro had maxed out, it checked another, redundant gyro—and got the same result. So began a cascading sequence of events, which included lots of back-and-forth between onboard computers. Then when that didn't help, it switched to a backup computer. And so forth. When all else failed, it stopped and went back to the top of the list—in modern terms, it rebooted.

Casani could picture it in his head. They had been clever in this design; they knew that *Voyager* had a long, cold, and dark trip ahead. New double-axis gyros had been selected and the software was cutting-edge, as was the computer hardware created by GE to JPL's exacting specifications. But what they had not thought of was that the rate at which the rocket was twisting would send *Voyager*'s brain into spasms. They would have to account for that next time.

SOLUTION:

Using flight-proven components, build a computer with the minimum complexity—and least fragility—that will get the job done. Try to think of everything that it might encounter, and when you find a mistake, fix it!

These lessons and others were rapidly incorporated into software patches for the other Voyager spacecraft, *Voyager 1*, sitting atop its own Titan at the Cape. This Voyager would follow a faster path to Jupiter; hence the reverse numerical order of launch. In a feat of round-the-clock efforts not dissimilar to the *Skylab* launch malfunctions, the still-Earthbound *Voyager 1* was updated in every way possible in preparation for launch. It had its own issues, including an upper stage that had to burn longer to compensate for an unexpectedly early shutdown of the Titan main stage, but the cybernetic drama of *Voyager 2* was not repeated. Score one for rapid implementation of lessons learned.

A TINY BRAIN

When referring to *Voyager*'s "computer," the term seems almost quaint. True, it was a binary-driven computing machine, but it was a distant relative of the processors that we are surrounded by today. It used three computers, each of which sported four *kilobytes* of rewritable memory. *Voyager*'s computer also had to be reprogrammable from the ground once it was in space, and it was expected to be operating for a decade or more (or, as it has turned out, for more than 35 years!). A tall order indeed.

The probe would also need to record data from its passes by Jupiter and the other planets for later transmission back to Earth. For this it used a spiffed-up version of an eight-track tape recorder, not terribly dissimilar from the one in your father's 1968 Ford. With this primitive storage and its basic computer about 1/100,000 the computing power of an 8-gig iPod. In today's world, it would barely qualify as a calculator—and yet, near the outer boundary of our solar system, this machine continues to function well into the twenty-first century.

In 1978, the Voyagers were state of the art. Casani and his fellow engineers had labored long and hard to make sure that these spacecraft—two of the first self-aware and reprogrammable machines ever to fly in space—would complete their long missions. *Voyager 1* would be the first of the pair to reach Jupiter and Saturn, following in the footsteps of the tiny *Pioneer 10* and *11* spacecraft, which had been sent out just a few years previously. But the Pioneers were very rudimentary machines, with very basic science loads and a tiny, low-resolution imager. Voyager brought a whole new level of sophistication to the game, lofting hugely improved cameras and sensing devices, and representing a quantum leap in science capabilities.

Once *Voyager 1* charted the two largest worlds in our solar system, it would head for interstellar space, the void between stars. *Voyager 2* would take a slower route to the outer solar system, passing Jupiter and Saturn as well, but also visiting Uranus and even Neptune. Together, planets make up about 99 percent of the mass in the solar system and were largely unexplored at the time. What little was known about Jupiter's Great Red Spot and Saturn's magnificent rings had not changed much in decades, and this one mission would magnify that knowledge a thousandfold. It was to be a grand sweep, taking in all the planets beyond Mars except Pluto (which would soon be demoted from planethood anyway).

RECLAIMING THE "GRAND TOUR"

The *Voyager 2* mission was what remained of an earlier mission design called the Grand Tour. As it turns out, every couple of hundred years, the outer planets align in such a way that a sequential flyby is possible, Jupiter–Saturn–Uranus–Neptune. But the Grand Tour mission was deemed too expensive, with its massive twin spacecraft and enormous fuel requirements, and it was shelved.

Voyager was created with what remained of the Grand Tour budget. Doing more with less, as they so often seem to, the engineers at JPL tried to salvage what they could—and did so magnificently.

CHALLENGE:

Take advantage of a unique planetary alignment with a gutted budget and build a spacecraft that can survive the worst conditions in the solar system.

In the end, the *Voyager 2* mission accomplished most of what the Grand Tour had intended. This was a result of a lot of innovative thinking and some risk taking on the part of JPL engineers, but it paid off. Not only were they able to visit the great gas giants of our solar system, but they were able, through pinpoint-accurate trajectory planning, to take close looks at many of the larger moons of these distant worlds as well.

While getting there would be one thing; surviving once they arrived was another. Pioneer had shown that the radiation hazards of the outer solar system were far more severe than had been predicted, and the more sophisticated Voyagers would need hardened electronics, much like those designed to survive nuclear war. So in what would become standard practice for JPL in the future, the lab borrowed a few tricks from the U.S. military's Cold War playbook and battle-hardened the brains on both Voyagers. Besides burying sensitive components deep inside the protective chassis of the craft, they actually capped individual transistors and capacitors in metal sheathing. It saved weight and protected the components.

SOLUTION:

Learning from previous missions into deep space, design within minimum specs to accomplish the desired tasks. Armor components and protect critical areas as simply—and as lightly—as possible.

And then there was the issue of navigating billions of miles of space. Performing close flybys of these huge, gravitationally grabby planets was an endeavor that needed to be planned with the utmost precision. Then JPL upped the ante by planning to fly past a number of Jupiter's and Saturn's moons. Those autonomous, reprogrammable computers would need to be updated frequently, and also be in regular communication with Earth. That would be no small feat in itself.

A FLICKERING CANDLE

Communicating with the Voyagers in the outer solar system would be like looking at a flickering candle in New York from atop a tall building in Seattle. That's how weak the signal would be when *Voyager 1* reached Jupiter, its first target, which averaged 500 million miles away. That's quite a reach when you are looking for a spacecraft that has a radio dish only 14 feet in diameter. It transmitted at 23 watts—today's cell phones cover about five miles with 3 watts, so at a half-billion miles away, the radio operated at a whisper.

Then, each increment past Jupiter made it exponentially harder. That flickering candle flame had moved, metaphorically, from Manhattan out to the moon. But you can pack just so much transmitter power into a small spacecraft, and the farther it needs to fly, the less weight it can carry. The Voyagers would have to be very efficient, and the Earth-based listening and transmitting operation very clever. By the time *Voyager 2* reached Uranus, it would be traveling in darkness, illuminated with just 1/400 of the sunlight we experience on Earth. The radio signals diminished in a similar way.

CHALLENGE:

Track and communicate with a spacecraft with a tiny radio that will travel billions of miles away from Earth.

To fill this kind of need, JPL had begun pitching the idea of a set of large Earth-based radio dishes, called the Deep Space Network, about the same time that NASA itself was created, in 1958. The pitch to Congress had been pretty simple: you need this for manned spaceflight; we need this for everything we plan to do. This was in a time just after the *Sputnik* "emergency," and the government was tuned in to all things space—the United States must not fall any further behind the Soviet Union. The effort was funded, and soon ground was broken for the Goldstone tracking dish out in the high desert of California. Two other large dishes were built near Canberra, Australia, and Johannesburg, South Africa, with Madrid, Spain added later. Between them, continuous coverage could be maintained with a spacecraft near the moon, or heading off to other planets.

SOLUTION:

Design and build a globe-girdling complex of interconnected radio dishes that can act in unison to find and follow the tiny flickering signal from *Voyager* and other distant spacecraft.

But communicating was just a part of the flying-to-Jupiter puzzle. The spacecraft also had to be aimed. Precision pointing at Jupiter from Earth is tough—the margin of error for the Voyager mission design, the size of its target corridor, if you will, *after* the spacecraft had traveled about 500 million miles, was . . . about 60 miles. That was threading the needle in a way that had never before been attempted; the *Pioneer 10* and *11* flights had had much larger margins. And it was not simply point-and-shoot, either. The gravitational fields of the planets it would pass were not completely mapped, and variations in solar wind could alter the spacecraft's course during the long journey out to Jupiter and beyond. And of course, they would have to account for changing weight as the probe burned off its fuel along the way.

As the trajectory was updated, occasional course corrections would be needed. Most of these could not be preprogrammed because as the Voyagers flew further from Earth, any trajectory angles would become magnified. Navigational corrections would have to incorporate any "drift" from the 60-mile-wide target. Commands would be sent up, and the craft would be told how long to burn the rocket motor for each maneuver, and in what direction. The burns could range from a few minutes to hours.

TRUSTING YOUR DESIGN

But in order to do this, *Voyager* had to rotate its high-gain antenna away from Earth. The ship would depend on its autonomous computer to perform the maneuver. It would also count on its gyroscopes to maintain proper orientation before and during the burn, then rotate the high-gain antenna back toward where it thought Earth should be. It was a white-knuckle experience for the controllers that would be repeated a number of times. Each time, the ship was older and farther away, and the transit times for commands—and verifications of success—were much, much longer. It's a graph that moves in the wrong direction. As the craft gets older and tireder, it has more malfunctions, less fuel, and less power, but is also much farther away and is expected to do increasingly more with less functional equipment. It is a testament to *Voyager*'s masters that they had the faith in their equipment, software, and management to take this risk multiple times, and that they were always ultimately successful. Sometimes the burns were absolutely necessary; other times they were to pick up better signal performance from the spacecraft or a closer approach to a target. But they always worked.

There was one more requirement to be fulfilled by the harried designers: how to communicate with any alien species that might come across the probe in interstellar space hundreds, thousands, or even millions of years after its departure from Earth. It was a fun intellectual exercise that got people thinking. The solution, after input from a board of scientists and futurists chaired by Carl Sagan, was to create a metallic *phonograph record*. This platter contained more than 100 digitized images and sounds of Earth, greetings from the president of the United States and the secretary general of the United Nations, various music samples (including Mozart and Chuck Berry), further greetings in 56 languages, some basic scientific laws, an illustration of human DNA for reference. Finally, a phonograph cartridge, needle, and instructions for playing the record were attached (if you are under 45, ask your parents).

After their launches in 1977, both spacecraft had flown past Jupiter as planned. John Casani, now in charge of the Galileo Jupiter orbiter, was rightfully proud of the twin spacecraft of which so much had been expected. The science was spectacular, creating vast amounts of data that would keep the scientists busy for decades. But perhaps even more amazing were the Voyagers' reconnaissance of moons that orbited Jupiter.

The four moons that could be easily observed from Earth (and had in fact been first observed by Galileo himself) were Ganymede, Callisto, Io, and Europa. The last two turned out to be the most remarkable. These were just four of the dozens that were ultimately discovered, but they turned out to be remarkable worlds of vastly differing characters.

Europa, which is nearly the same size as Earth's moon, had a remarkably flat surface riddled by cracks and fissures. What it did not have was craters, which put it at odds with virtually every other rocky planet or moon in the solar system. The final conclusion was that there is a huge ocean of water—much like Earth's oceans—beneath an icy crust. This was a stunner; nothing of this kind had been predicted out in the icy spaces beyond the "Goldilocks zone," where planets are warm enough to have liquid water. The obvious conclusion was that Europa was so twisted, pumped, and battered by Jupiter's gravitational forces that it generated enough heat to keep water a liquid beneath its icy crust. And where there is liquid water, there may be life. That hypothesis awaits another probe to land and sample below the ice.

A FINAL, REMARKABLE DISCOVERY AT JUPITER

And then there was incredible Io. A young woman on the navigational team, Linda Moribito, was studying pictures of the Jovian moons shortly after they had been downloaded and processed. Even before *Voyager* reached Jupiter, 16 moons had been discovered from Earth-bound telescopes and indirect observation. By the time the Voyagers and later Galileo missions had run their course, the count was up to 67. All the large ones were interesting in their own right, but it was Io that held Linda's interest at the moment.

She noticed something odd about the picture. There was a small bulge off to one side of Io. She looked and looked, and realized that what she was seeing was a volcano erupting. This was a first on many levels: the first real-time geological activity observed on any moon in the solar system, the first direct evidence of active volcanism on another world, and much more. She was stunned.

Over time, nine eruptions were noted from *Voyager 1*'s flyby of Io. The possibility that enormous tidal forces from Jupiter might squeeze and flex the moon sufficiently to cause interior heating, which in turn could result in volcanic activity, had been predicted before. But rarely does reality fit the predictions so nicely. It was a stunning development, and by the time the images were properly adjusted and enhanced, the images of Io looked like a huge cosmic pizza with fountains of icy liquids spewing forth. The world, already dumbstruck by the fantastic images of Jupiter, was once more amazed.

The Voyagers, alone and uncaring, rushed on to Saturn.

NO ROOM FOR ERROR

As the twin craft left the Jovian system, the challenges increased. They were still operating in a similarly sized navigational corridor, but the distances were becoming far vaster, and the radio signals now took many hours to complete the round trip. But perhaps most concerning was the fact that the Voyagers had been affected by their trip past Jupiter and had been slung onward by its massive gravitational field, second only to the sun's. This field, while *generally* understood, was still somewhat of an unknown. And because this was a flyby, not an orbital mission, it was important to get the angles right when they exited Jupiter's space. Minor errors here would cost dearly in fuel later to correct any trajectory errors. A popular analogy for the required accuracy at the time was teeing off a golf ball in Manhattan and sinking a hole-in-one in Los Angeles, minus any wind that might be encountered. Oh, and the spacecraft would be traveling away from Jupiter at 60,000 miles per hour.

Voyager 1, although launched second, had taken an even faster trajectory to reach Jupiter. It flew through the dangerous high-intensity radiation belts, running its instruments and snapping pictures all the while. It also mapped radiation levels, gravitational pull, magnetic fields, and much more. As the mission planners on the ground built up an increasingly detailed map of Jupiter's neighborhood, they would take those data and make better, more detailed plans for *Voyager 2*. Returning the favor, *Voyager 2* was able to track incoming "storm fronts" of solar radiation and pass that news to the ground for inclusion into *Voyager 1*'s plans. So for the planets that the two probes had in common, Jupiter and Saturn and their many moons, they were able to build on each other's experiences.

Along the way, each spacecraft suffered its share of technological drama. These malfunctions demanded quick, yet careful responses. If they occurred during a cruise phase, there was much more time to correct or compensate for them. If they occurred near an encounter with a planet or moon, there was much less. Each problem would need a carefully considered response. This response must be designed, tested on ground-based duplicate equipment (a *Voyager 2.5*, if you will), then packaged for transmission and delivered to the spacecraft. Great care had to be taken to not make things worse or to create additional issues. It was innovation on the fly.

Before reaching Jupiter, *Voyager 2*'s primary radio began to falter. Exactly why was not clear, but there was a redundant unit onboard, so the controllers switched the backup. That worked for a time, then the backup started having issues of its own. The radios had been designed with an electronic circuit that would filter incoming radio transmissions by their wavelengths. As the spacecraft moved away from Earth, a shift in radio frequency would occur, and it would drop. We have all experienced similar phenomena, known as Doppler shifts, when a train speeds by blowing its horn, and as it passes, the tone drops. Radio waves do the same thing, but in this case the stakes were higher. *Voyager 2*'s radio was failing to adjust for this shift in frequency and was becoming increasingly deaf.

CHALLENGE:

How to "fix" failing components on a probe hundreds of millions of miles away.

The problem was that a single capacitor had failed—one tiny, inexpensive component, but, like so many, a critical one. By now the main radio was completely dead, so to save the mission, they needed a fix for the backup unit. After careful calculations of changing speeds, they were able to devise a system by which the outgoing signal (for *Voyager 2* only) was artificially shifted in frequency to simulate what the probe would be expecting with its failed filter. In effect, they fibbed to the radio so that it would allow the commands to be heard. The sticky part was that as the craft continued on its mission, speeds would change each time it passed a planet. At Jupiter alone, *Voyager 2* would approach at a speed of just under 30,000 mph. After passing the planet, it would depart at almost 54,000 mph. The speed would have nearly doubled. The Doppler shift would increase, and it was a constantly accelerating target. It was one huge migraine of a math and engineering problem, and it is a profound example of why engineers must take calculus.

SOLUTION:

Utilizing redundant and parallel hardware, design workarounds and bypasses using other systems. Test these procedures extensively before committing to them in space.

This was only the first of many situations in which accommodations would be made on the ground to nurse the aging robots along. As the mission stretched on across the decades, intensive reprogramming was uplinked and increasingly compressed signals downlinked to keep twin spacecraft functioning as they aged and moved farther into space.

SAILING PAST SATURN

On November 12, 1980, *Voyager 1* made its kamikaze dash past Saturn, flying just 77,000 miles above the icy methane clouds below. The probe had been directed into a path that slung it away from the ecliptic, the equatorial plane of the solar system, and off into the empty reaches. This was done to facilitate a closer look at Titan, Saturn's largest moon, which had the distinction of being the only moon anywhere known to have a significant atmosphere.

While there was not much to see visually through Titan's thick, toxic clouds, many other valuable measurements were made. Titan was later found to have small oceans of hydrocarbons (essentially bodies of gasoline) and many weather-formed surface features similar to those found on Earth.

As *Voyager 1* sped toward the edge of the solar system, *Voyager 2* headed off toward Neptune and Uranus. These icy methane-rich worlds, resplendent in their deep blue hues, are forever cloaked in cold and darkness. The spacecraft reached Uranus in 1986, nearly two billion miles from the sun with an orbital cycle of 86 years, and farther from Saturn than Saturn is from Earth.

By this time, the data rate was down to the equivalent of the Internet's dial-up days, and the one-way radio time delay was 2 hours, 40 minutes. From JPL's point of view, designing and controlling *Voyager 2*'s planetary flybys was getting more and more challenging, and both spacecraft were just getting older and more creaky.

Voyager 2 discovered 11 new moons and charted the Uranian system as it flew by. Unique to that world was the tilt of its axis—almost 90 degrees from North as seen from Earth. This results in a magnetic field that is shaped like a giant corkscrew trailing outward from the planet.

Also of note were observations of the moon Miranda. Its surface was a hodgepodge of geological nightmares, apparently from some ancient event that resulted in Miranda's being smashed up and reassembling itself back into the moon that we see today. It is unique in the solar system.

Finally, a ring system was seen around Uranus, not dissimilar to that surrounding Saturn, although much, much less spectacular. By the time the spacecraft had left the system, it had passed its targets within *16 miles* of JPL's aiming point.

As *Voyager 1* continued its journey to the outer reaches of the solar system, *Voyager 2* left Uranus and headed to its final destination, Neptune. The outermost of the planets (Pluto has since been demoted to a "dwarf planet"), Neptune swam into view three years later in 1989. After passing the planet, the spacecraft headed off to Neptune's moon Triton as its final destination. The data brought down from the spacecraft at this distance were about one-billionth of a watt in strength, truly a flickering match in the darkness.

Notable discoveries included Neptune's "Great Dark Spot" (long since vanished), and a frigid atmosphere similar in makeup to that of Uranus. After passing the planet, *Voyager 2* exited the area heading south of the ecliptic, heading generally in the opposite trajectory from its sibling.

THIRTY-FIVE YEARS LATER . . .

Remarkably, the mission of Voyager continues onward through the farthest, darkest, and coldest reaches of known space. Now, some 35 years after it encountered Saturn, *Voyager 1* has left the solar system. Scientists' models of that boundary had been based on theory and guesswork as much as on observation, and they envisioned a fairly simple boundary between the inside and outside of the solar system "bubble." But it has turned out to be more complex than that, and it took some time to deduce when the aging spacecraft actually exited the heliosphere.

CHALLENGE:

Preserving a mission that has gone well beyond all expectations of achievements . . . and budgets.

Today, the twin Voyager spacecraft are monitored and controlled from a building about a mile from JPL. There was simply no room at the main campus, so NASA moved the control complex offsite. It's a cluster of low-slung offices that are as plain as plain can be. Entering Voyager Mission Control, you would be excused if you failed to notice that this was the nerve center of the first space mission to the stars. If it weren't for the occasional schematic and posters of Jupiter and Saturn thumbtacked to the walls, it would look like any other slightly careworn industrial park office. But it is what is demanded by NASA's slim budgets in the twenty-first century.

At the center of the space are a few long tables with older Sun workstations running the vintage software that keeps the Voyagers alive. They are checked daily, but only a few times a month are major operations performed. The Voyagers, both many billions of miles away, are largely self-sufficient, even after all this time.

NASA still downloads data from the spacecraft on a daily basis for a few hours per day using large tracking dishes. The stream includes engineering data—basically the health-trace of the spacecraft—plus other data collected at the rim of the solar system. The cameras have long since been turned off, so it's a nonvisual experience.

SOLUTION:

Trim required personnel, equipment, and "mission footprint" to a bare minimum, and use only the time and personnel that are absolutely necessary to accomplish the task at hand.

Voyager 2 continues its lonely journey, traveling a bit more slowly than *Voyager 1*. In about 300,000 years, it will pass near the star Sirius. By 2025, however, its power systems will have degenerated to the point that it will no longer be able to communicate with Earth, and it will be shut down, to continue its trek silent and cold.

Voyager 1 is the furthest functioning emissary of Earth in existence, but it too will face severe power shortages in the same time range, about 2025. In February of 1990, its cameras looked back toward Earth and, in one of its last shots, it took a picture now known as the "Pale Blue Dot," with Earth tiny and insignificant in the vast blackness. In 2011, it entered a region termed by NASA as "cosmic purgatory," the area where instrument readings from the sun are roughly balanced by those from interstellar space. It's headed toward a star called Gliese 445 and will pass that system in about 40,000 years.

John Casani is retired now and living in Pasadena, not far from JPL. While tending to his garden or working on his son's house, both of which he still does vigorously in his early eighties, he often thinks back on the great voyages of exploration with which he was involved. Back in 1977, shortly after the Voyagers were launched, he was chosen to head the Galileo mission to Jupiter, and later Cassini to Saturn. But Voyager was special, for as the aging twin spacecraft straddle the edge of our solar system, they mark the beginning of our long journey to the stars.

INNOVATIONS

- Created a computer that not only could function without input for increasing periods of time, but was programmable and would actually stop and search for Earth if it sensed something wrong.
- Created twin spacecraft that would survive not just the primary mission of scouting the outer planets, but even exiting the solar system almost 40 years later.
- Navigated billions of miles from Earth and hit targets less than 20 miles wide.
- Created a phonograph record containing messages from many of the countries of Earth, as well as depictions of its people—and a needle to play it with.

- Created a multination coalition of tracking stations and operated them continuously for more than 50 years.
- Maintained technical proficiency to operate, maintain, and repair hardware and software more than four decades after its design.
- Created a management and funding apparatus (frequently threatened with budget cuts) to maintain a program that outlived its primary mission by 25 years.

CHAPTER 15

COMPROMISE 101: THE SPACE SHUTTLE—DOING MORE FOR LESS

CHALLENGES

- Design and build a successor to the Apollo program, creating new hardware that is reusable.
- Reduce the cost of access to orbit by a sizable factor.
- Provide rapid turnaround of this launch service.
- Scale back plans for reusability because of budget considerations without losing capability.
- Provide the ability to bring cargo back to Earth as well as taking it into space.
- Manage a contractor network spread among over a dozen states.
- Recover from two major in-flight disasters during the program.
- Do all the above for much less than the cost of the Apollo program.

INNOVATION ON A BUDGET

It was not supposed to look like that. To the casual observer, of course, the problem was that the rocket was no longer symmetrical, as America's moon rockets had been—there was a huge airplane off to one side. To an observer in the know, it was more complex: the entire design was wrong. Thank the Nixon administration for that.

> **CHALLENGE:**
>
> Design and build a reusable spacecraft with slashed—and insufficient—budgets.

America's space shuttle, which flew for exactly 30 years, was a study in innovation that was backed into crippling budget constraints. Never again would any U.S. space project enjoy the open checkbook that had spawned Apollo. NASA's budget would be far smaller and always in contention. In the end, this would cost more than it saved.

The Space Transportation System, known to most of us as the STS or space shuttle, actually had its origins in World War II. The Germans had developed plans for a winged rocket plane that would ride atop an augmented version of their V2 rocket that would be boosted to just below orbit, skip off the upper atmosphere until it had crossed the Atlantic, then drop bombs (atomic ones, they hoped) on New York. That design, called the Silverbird, never made it past paper, but it was the starting point.

Then in the early 1960s, the U.S. Air Force concluded that it needed its own space program for defense purposes. The logical choice was an extension of the X-15, which was then flying research missions. The new design was to be the X-20, later dubbed project DynaSoar (for "dynamic soaring"). It consisted of what looked like a small, black space shuttle launched on top of a Titan booster. It would carry one to four Air Force astronauts and a military payload to orbit, then glide back to Earth when the mission was completed. But the U.S. government had its hands full with the Apollo program in the 1960s, and did not feel the need to fund two financially voracious efforts. DynaSoar was cancelled.

Flash forward to the 1970s: the Apollo program had been a resounding success, but it was expensive and somewhat single-purposed. It had been designed and built to go to the moon, and while there were plenty of design studies for follow-on missions, most of them did not fully utilize the amazing power of the Saturn V booster. At nearly a half-billion dollars each, the rocket was also deemed too expensive to continue to produce, so the assembly line was closed. An alternative program had been under study since the mid-1960s: a reusable spaceship that would reduce operating costs and allow for cheap and frequent access to space. And so the space shuttle was born.

But this was not the shuttle as we know it today. This early concept was for a *completely* reusable system. The orbiter, the winged part that we all know as the space shuttle itself, was the only facet of the original designs to reach fruition. The large orange fuel tank (the External Tank or ET) and its two solid rocket boosters (or SRBs) replaced what should have been another large winged aircraft. It would have a second crew of two pilots, and after it had been launched and had carried the shuttle toward orbit, it would have separated from the orbiter and flown back to the launch site for refurbishment and reuse. The shuttle itself would continue into orbit, much as the shuttle orbiter we know today did.

ENTER THE AIR FORCE—AGAIN

As the designs progressed, an unwelcome player reentered the arena. The Air Force was back, and since it had never managed to get its own manned space program off the ground, it decided to join with

NASA in specifying what a new shuttle should do. This vastly complicated the design process, as the space plane would now have to be capable of placing satellites into polar orbits (north-to-south instead of the traditional equatorial), and would also need what is called cross-range ability, that is, the ability to fly well off the equator. This would necessitate bigger, delta-shaped wings, a larger rudder, and more. And the size of the payload bay in the final design, not by coincidence, matched the large spy satellites that were then in use. It was all just more flies in the ointment.

As Apollo wound down in the early 1970s, the Nixon administration made it clear that it would not support the heavy investment a fully reusable design would require. It would have needed substantial innovation and R&D to reach fruition, and this would cost money—lots of it. The administration wanted a cheaper and simpler design, yet one that retained reusability, or at least partial reusability. This would be critical to getting budget approval. As a result, NASA created the shuttle as it flew for 30 years.

The resulting program is a study in reverse or perhaps inverse innovation: backing off from a robust and ultimately cheaper and safer design to fit financial and political realities (certainly not the first or the last time that this will beset a government-procured high-tech program). The grand idea of a fully reusable shuttle was jammed into a budget-constrained box. The results were less than optimal.

Pushing back, NASA embarked on a PR campaign—it was the only way to assure continued funding. The space shuttle was now marketed to Congress as a "space truck"—able to supply easy, cheap, and frequent access to space with a reusable spacecraft (exactly how much would be reusable was an open question). Cargo rates to orbit would drop from $1,000 per pound to perhaps $15 per pound—an exponential savings. The flight schedule was projected at an unbelievable once per week, with a cost of about $3 million per flight. The shuttle would fuel up, fly, complete a mission, land, be serviced and refueled, and fly again. Both civilian and military payloads could be accommodated in the huge payload bay, and it could fly upon demand. There was even an Air Force–operated launch complex being constructed on the U.S. West Coast at Vandenberg Air Force Base. And with four orbiters in the fleet, there would always be one that was ready to trundle off to a launchpad. Simple.

That was the plan. The reality would be nothing like it.

SOLUTION:

Back away from previous ambitious plans and use existing technology where possible. To maintain funding, overpromise future cost savings.

THE CHALLENGE OF REUSABILITY

While the overall design was being hammered out, work began on the rocket engines. The orbiter would need at least three of them, and they would have to be reusable as well. To date, the only rocket engine of any size that had been truly reused was that of the X-15. That rocket engine could fly between 20 and 50 missions before refurbishment. These flights were just a few minutes at a time, though. The shuttle would need engines—running on much more powerful fuels—that could fly 100 times with a 10-hour burn-time lifespan (that does not sound like much, but in rocket terms, it's a huge number). All this was supposed to occur with minimal maintenance and refurbishment. The task was assigned to Rocketdyne in Canoga Park, California, the builders of the magnificent F-1 engines that powered the Saturn V.

Rocketdyne approached the challenge with dogged determination. From the Apollo program, it had experience in building engines that ran off the powerful combined fuels of liquid hydrogen and liquid oxygen. The engineers felt confident that they could produce an SSME (space shuttle main engine) that could meet these objectives.

And so they designed, built, and tested a few new engine designs. And they tested, and tested. Explosions were not infrequent, and the schedule slipped badly, as did much of the shuttle development. It soon became clear that their Apollo/Saturn V experience was a far cry from the thrust and reliability needed to power a space shuttle. For one thing, the new engine would have to operate at internal pressures four to five times as high as the Apollo-era engines. Specific parts of the engine would experience pressures as much as eight times as high.

Then there was the issue of reentry heating. The X-15 had absorbed the heat of reentry and transmitted it through the structure of the craft, while the pilot stayed cool in an isolated, cooled cockpit. This would not work for the shuttle for a variety of reasons, including the demands of passenger accommodation and cargo as well as the huge size. On the other end of the engineering spectrum, the Apollo spacecraft had come hurtling back from the moon at 25,000 mph with what were known as "ablative" heat shields. These structures, made of resin and various plastics, burned away as the capsule slammed through the atmosphere, shedding heat as the shield slowly charred and evaporated. In effect, the burnt by-products carried the heat away. But these were by their very nature a one-shot deal, and they could burn unevenly, becoming less aerodynamic in the process. They would not do for a shuttle.

CHALLENGE:

Protecting the orbiter's fragile aluminum airframe from the scorching heat of reentry while saving weight.

The solution was to create lightweight ceramic surfaces that would rapidly absorb and shed heat. In theory, this would work well for most of the ship—thousands of them, a few inches on each side. These tiles were made from silica, the same material used to create glassware. But in this case, the silica was whipped up like a ceramic smoothie while it was still hot, hardening into a glass sponge. Then the heat-facing side had a smooth shell-like surface applied to it. It was eggshell-thin, but if heated to white hot, it could cool (or shed the heat) within a few seconds. If it had any drawback, it was its fragility—you could crack it with a firm rap of the knuckles. But it was an otherwise miraculous invention. Almost 25,000 of these were glued to the surface of the orbiter.

For areas of extreme heating, like the leading edges of the wing and the nose of the spacecraft, newly developed carbon composites would suffice. These had layers of carbon-fiber mats laid up in a mold, similar to the way Chevy Corvettes were made at the time. But in this case, the entire structure was heated until the fiber mats *pyrolized*—basically, they were preburned. The resulting material could withstand up to 4,000 degrees of heat. Other parts of the orbiter that faced less heating were covered in cloth (a variation of a heat-resisting fabric called Nomex) in large sheets. And, of course, the bottom was covered in a patchwork of small and fragile ceramic tiles. How well they would work in practice was an open question. Such tiles had never been tried on this scale.

SOLUTION:

Use finesse, not brute force. Instead of metal armor, develop thin, feather-light ceramic tiles that shed heat as quickly as it develops.

A huge challenge was how to boost the shuttle into orbit. Ideas for the shuttle's booster included a flyable first stage with 12 of the new Rocketdyne engines that would carry the orbiter most of the way to space, detach, and land with its own auxiliary jet engines. Per-flight costs were now estimated at about $6 million. There were now to be upwards of 60 flights per year.

CHALLENGE:

How to reduce spiraling costs and spacecraft mass.

As the budget available for shuttle development continued to shrink, a major decision was made that would drastically alter the path of the program. With a fully reusable design utilizing a flyback first stage, the fuel that the orbiter would need in order to continue into space would have to be held in tanks enclosed within the shuttle itself. This increased the orbiter's size and weight, and the amount of surface area that had to be protected from heating. The simple solution was to design an external tank that could be dropped once it reached orbit. This would mean that that the system would not be entirely reusable, and those tanks would cost money. But it was a save now/pay later scheme that was unavoidable, and it signaled a move toward an only half-reusable system. This was the largest, and ultimately most costly, compromise made by NASA.

In the final design, all the liquid fuel would be carried in a huge external tank. This allowed the remaining expensive part of the system, the orbiter, to be shrunk yet again. Without the need to carry bulky liquid hydrogen and liquid oxygen, the orbiter was now basically a crew cockpit and cargo bay enclosed in an aerodynamic shell. It was like a jet airliner without large fuel tanks—just people and payload and a set of small maneuvering engines to adjust its orbit. And the up-front cost was also much cheaper, much to the glee of the folks over at Nixon's Office of Management and Budget.

SOLUTION:

Compromise reusability and discard heavy fuel tanks as the shuttle ascends into space. The upside: reduced development costs. The downside: higher operating costs.

But even as NASA delivered these cost-conscious concessions, budget trimming continued to run the wrong way on the graph when lined up against even this more modest set of funding goals. With the cancellation of the manned first stage, NASA needed another way to get the shuttle off the ground—the three main engines would not have nearly enough thrust. Something with the power of the abandoned Saturn V was needed, but it had to be cheap.

CHALLENGE:

Much more boost is needed, but the funds required to develop a sophisticated new rocket booster are unavailable.

Wernher von Braun and his team of German engineers and designers (the booster team) asserted that liquid-fueled booster rockets were the safest approach. They could be throttled or even shut down in an emergency, and they had infinite flexibility. This is why Huntsville had been supporters of various flyback booster designs. Now that this was off the table, but a massive initial thrust was still needed to get this cobbled-together shuttle off the pad and on its way to orbit, the engineers were forced to accept an ultimately deadly compromise: huge solid rockets.

DEADLY COMPROMISE

Since the Chinese began designing skyrockets a millennium ago, solid rockets had been a mainstay of rocket science. Many military applications favored them: they stored well, needed little preparation, and gave a lot of bang for the buck. But von Braun had never favored them for manned spaceflight (except for emergency rockets and small auxiliary boosters). The main issue was this: once ignited, they could not be stopped. They would burn until they had expended all their fuel. That is why, when the *Challenger* broke up in 1986, even though the shuttle itself was falling in pieces toward the ocean, the solid rocket boosters, or SRBs, continued to fire and go their own way until they were destroyed by the Air Force range safety officer.

But it appeared that the shuttle would have to use solid boosters given the financial constraints and ever-nearing flight dates. Bowing to the inevitable, NASA signed a contract with Morton Thiokol (now ATK) in Utah to build huge solid rockets that would provide more than 80 percent of the thrust for the spacecraft during the first few minutes of flight. Twelve feet in diameter and 150 feet high, they were a major evolution in solid rocket design. Each was made up of four sections, joined with a fitted joint and O-rings (which are what burned through when the *Challenger* was lost). The case was heavily built. When it had finished hurling the orbiter and the external tank toward orbit, it would be cut loose to parachute into the Atlantic and be picked up by a NASA tugboat. Once it had been hauled back, it would be refurbished and refueled, supposedly cutting costs.

SOLUTION:

Engineer the largest solid-fueled rocket in history—essentially a huge skyrocket. Make the casing rugged enough to withstand recovery and reuse.

Along with the orbiter and its engines, the SRBs became the only other reusable part of the shuttle. The huge external tank would break up in the atmosphere. Still, this meant that three-quarters of the overall shuttle "stack" was reusable. That was a good thing, right? Well, it should have been, but this was a case where theory and practice diverged markedly..

And then there were those SSMEs, the main engines. These were an evolution of both the giant F-1 and smaller J-2 (upper-stage) engines from the Saturn V. The problems were similar, but they were magnified by two things: first, although the engine was smaller than the F-1, all the operating pressures were much higher, the fuel temperatures colder, and the tolerances finer. More performance had to be wrung from a smaller, more stressed package.

As usual for such an undertaking, engines and engine components failed on the stand. A few of them blew up, but that was part of the learning curve. The worst of it was when a liquid oxygen turbopump failed. It was a high-pressure, high-speed component that went from zero to 28,000 rpm in a matter of seconds. It was also high-pressure, up to 4,400 psi, and it was running ultra-cold cryogenic fuels through it. The combination tended to make metal brittle and cause lubricants to freeze. The high revolutions made the turbine blades fly off their mounts and shatter the casing, which they did with some regularity for a time. There was often not enough of the engine left to discover what had gone wrong, and a lot of indirect detective work had to be done.

The engines contained more than 45,000 parts. Exotic metals were combined in equally exotic ways to handle the huge temperature differentials and high pressures. Over time, Rocketdyne got a handle on the SSME and wrestled it into compliance. In a final analysis of the shuttle program, this troublesome component, which had been a "pacing item" for some time (in that it was holding back overall development) turned out to be one of the most reliable parts of the shuttle system. Though there was one in-flight shutdown (which did not affect the mission) and a number of launch delays associated with these engines, no SSME ever failed catastrophically. And the average engine flew 135 missions, with three engines used per flight. That's 405 single engine uses with about *58 hours* of total burn time. Not bad for an item that had been regularly decorating a few acres of desert with white-hot chunks of shrapnel a few years before.

Not so the SRBs. While the large rocket boosters tested well, it took only one failure to kill astronauts. Few who saw it will forget that awful day on January 28, 1986, when a burn-through of rubber O-rings on an SRB section section joint caused *Challenger* to explode, killing all seven souls aboard.

In the final review of Thiokol's design, it was noted that the joints between case sections had excessive play and tended to open up when the rocket lifted off because of forces exerted when it left the pad. Furthermore, the O-ring material became very brittle in the cold—it had been 28 degrees Fahrenheit when *Challenger* launched to its doom. This poor response to cold was aptly demonstrated when Dr. Richard Feynman of Caltech, who was on the accident review board, immersed a piece of the material in ice water. Removing it, he demonstrated that it had become hard as a rock—it could no longer seal the SRB joint. The video of this brilliant demonstration still impresses today, and it was a major embarrassment to both NASA and Thiokol. As Feynman put it, "Reality must take precedence over public relations, for nature cannot be fooled." In a hasty redesign, Thiokol added a third O-ring and a "capture joint," a metal hook that kept the sections from spreading too much under stress. It should have been there all along.

And then there was the heat shield—the "Thermal Protection System"—that ultimately resulted in the shuttle's being nicknamed "the flying brickyard." NASA's decision to go with heat-resistant ceramic tiles instead of heat-shedding metal alloys may have saved money up front, but it continued to bite the agency in its nether regions for decades afterward. The tile and composites system worked, but it was incredibly delicate. As the shuttle hurtled through the atmosphere during the launch phase, bits of insulation sometimes rained down from the external tank and the whole craft experienced massive vibrations, both of which could cause tile damage or loss. Falling insulation caused the second major shuttle failure when *Columbia* broke up during reentry in 2003. There were other dangers to the tiles too—as the shuttle boosted away from Earth, even raindrops could become a deadly enemy: at certain speeds, water drops are as hard as metal pellets and could puncture the tiles. All in all, the system was effective, but it was expensive and more evolutionary than revolutionary. This was incremental innovation, crippled by underinvestment.

THE FINAL VERDICT

Clearly the shuttle was not the inexpensive "space truck" it had been represented as during the early years. After being promised as a cheap and reusable replacement for the "expensive" Apollo system, the shuttle proved to be anything but. Some of this was the result of compromises in the design required by shrinking budgets, and some was due to the fact that NASA had been wildly unrealistic about the technologies involved. There was also an institutional fixation on reusability. This was a far more complex and fragile system than Apollo had been, and this fact hobbled the program from day one. When the shuttle finally began flying in 1981, it was years behind schedule and grossly over budget. And while flying tests and transporting the orbiters to the Cape, it became clear that the tiles were a problem—they flew off as if they were held on by library paste. Millions were spent on trial-and-error solutions to the problem; ultimately it became a matter of better glue and careful inspection.

The shuttle ultimately flew 135 missions over 30 years, which was far fewer missions than had been intended (an average of 4.5 per year instead of the wished-for 60 missions). And this greatly reduced manifest was flown across twice as many years as the system had been meant to fly (30 instead of the planned 15 years).

But it is the cost that stuns, even today. The program was budgeted at a wildly optimistic $7.5 billion, which in today's dollars is more like $43 billion. The final cost in modern dollars? Almost

$200 billion. Early on, the program had predicted per-flight costs of as little as $5 or $6 million; this was later rounded up to about $30 to $40 million (in 1980s dollars). As you can see with some simple math, the actual cost per flight was closer to $1.5 *billion*—yes, that's with a B. In the final analysis, it might well have been far cheaper to keep the "expensive" Saturn V rocket of the Apollo era in production—with amortization across 135 missions, it could have saved a bundle. But that's not what happened.

It is easy to fault NASA for many of the space shuttle's shortcomings. It was too expensive, too fragile, and too dangerous. In the end, it killed 14 astronauts in flight-related accidents connected to both design flaws and poor management decisions. But it was by far the most complex machine ever designed and flown. It consisted of millions of parts, 230 miles of wire, and more than 1,060 individual plumbing connections, from the huge joints between the external tank and the orbiter to tiny cooling pipes. So if the major components were not truly revolutionary, it was a striking and monumental task of evolution that made this machine, the size of a small naval ship, fly at all.

The space shuttle built the International Space Station, deployed the Hubble Space Telescope, flew multiple repair missions to that and other satellites, visited and resupplied the Russian Mir space station, and flew thousands of experiments in material and biosciences. It was a remarkable machine that served as a three-decade bridge between Apollo and today, when we are seeing the rise of the private sector in spaceflight and NASA returning to an Apollo-like rocket and capsule design. And for now, U.S. astronauts flying to the space station must do so on the Russian Soyuz, a 50-year-old design that was originally intended to beat the United States to the moon. That's irony. For all its problems and limitations, the space shuttle is sorely missed. It was, for all its limitations, a machine well ahead of its time.

INNOVATIONS

- Created a reusable successor to Apollo, although with an ability greatly diminished from early plans.
- Maintained some elements of reusability.
- Managed 135 flights with increasingly old and worn equipment.
- Delivered dozens of payloads to orbit.
- Executed multiple captures and repairs of satellites in space.
- Assembled and supplied the International Space Station.
- Managed program recovery from (and congressional investigation of) two major in-flight disasters: *Challenger* in 1986 and *Columbia* in 2003.

Note: Most other program goals, such as affordability, reusability, and reduced launch cost, were not met.

CHAPTER 16

BUCK ROGERS: THE INTERNATIONAL SPACE STATION

CHALLENGES

- Create a permanent outpost in space, using the space shuttle as the primary delivery and servicing mechanism.
- Design components that can be assembled in orbit by the shuttle's and station's robotic arms and astronauts during extravehicular activity (EVA).
- Make the transition from a specifically American effort to an international endeavor, with numerous partners of differing abilities and financial resources.
- Maintain and lead this international partnership for at least three decades.
- After the cessation of shuttle flights, facilitate continued supply and support with a blend of international government and U.S. commercial flight providers.
- Prior to decommissioning of the space station in 2020, design and construct some kind of follow-on activities in orbit around Earth.

SPACE STATION? WHAT SPACE STATION?

Chat up the average American teenager and ask what NASA's most impressive achievement is. The answers may include some vague idea of a Mars rover, and most of them will know that humans landed on the moon at some time in the hazy past. Some will mention plans to send people to Mars, and still others think that we have already landed humans there. Clearly NASA's public relations could use an overhaul. But PR is not inherently a part of NASA's charter, and the resources available for the promotion of past accomplishments and future plans are severely limited at the best of times. In these times of federal scarcity, NASA's PR machine has lost momentum.

In the space race years, NASA's PR was simple: the commercial media did it. The major TV networks, all three of them, covered space. The major radio networks did the same. The nation's newspapers followed suit. Today, the situation is much more complex: the marketplace is huge and fragmented, and interest in space is just one of those fragments—and to most people, not a very sexy one at that.

Back to our teenager: his or her awareness of the space station, or of the benefits of that program, is likely to be small to nonexistent.

Public interest in the International Space Station, or ISS, and indeed NASA in general, seems to be at an all-time low. Point out that there is a football-field-sized Buck Rogers marvel whizzing overhead every 90 minutes at 17,000 miles per hour (mph) with up to six crew members aboard, and you will probably get a glimmer of a response: oh, yeah—it's there, it's working, and it must do something cool, right?

Clearly, the ISS has an image problem. Some feel that it also lacks a clearly defined mission. But it does not suffer from a lack of accomplishment.

STATIONS IN SPACE

Ideas of an orbital habitat date back to before the early twentieth century. A fiction writer envisioned an artificial "moon made of bricks" in 1870 (99 years before the first moon landing). In the twentieth century, thinkers in Russia and Germany wrote of enclosed vessels orbiting the Earth. By World War II, the Germans were considering a manned orbiting "sun gun" that would focus solar energy on a target 5,000 miles below. By the mid-1950s, Wernher von Braun suggested "the wheel," a huge wheel-shaped cylinder that would rotate, creating artificial gravity, and be staffed by Army personnel. In the late 1950s and early 1960s, the U.S. Air Force was trying to get into manned spaceflight and came up with a concept called the Manned Orbiting Laboratory or MOL, an orbital spy platform for keeping watch over the Soviets. The development of large, precision unmanned spy satellites made most of these ideas unnecessary.

By the early 1970s, the Soviet Union and the United States had each lofted small space stations. These worked well and were effective test beds for what was to come. In the 1980s, Russia flew Mir, its first large, sophisticated, and modular space station, and it operated for more than a decade.

Then it was once again America's turn. NASA wanted a large, modular, and robust space station that would outdo everything that had gone before. It ultimately got most of what it wanted, but not the way it had planned. The ISS was initially commissioned in 1984 by the Reagan administration as Space Station Freedom, and it soon included a limited roster of international partners. Japan was brought into the fold to contribute a research module, and Canada was given the task of building a manipulator arm, as it had done for the space shuttle. The European Space Agency folded its own plans for a station called Columbus into the ISS, and eventually provided a resupply ship as well. But it was the new Russian Federation that provided the lion's share of foreign technology.

CHALLENGE:

Build a large and permanent orbiting space station with NASA's ever-dwindling budgets.

It is this collaboration that may be the most innovative aspect of the ISS program. While many of the technologies are cutting edge, and the construction of the station via dozens of shuttle launches was impressively new and highly evolutionary, international cooperation in space on this level was a true revolution.

Prior to the ISS, the first international cooperation had been the oft-forgotten Apollo-Soyuz Test Project. In 1975, Russia launched a Soyuz spacecraft and America its last Apollo moonship, and the two linked up in orbit in a bit of early perestroika. Given that the Soviet Union was still in full flower, this was a truly impressive accomplishment, and it paved the way for future cooperation in space as intended, although not as anticipated.

During the 1980s, NASA and the European Space Agency collaborated on a laboratory module that flew in the shuttle's payload bay, which foreshadowed ESA's design of space station components. Then, in 1993, Vice President Al Gore met with Russian Prime Minister Viktor Chernomyrdin, and the two laid out an early framework for what was to become the largest and most expensive example of multinational cooperation in history. This meeting also primed the use of the space shuttle to dock with the Russian station Mir to test cooperative systems to be used in the ISS. While relations between the two countries since then have been mixed, their cooperation in space has been exemplary.

The station had been part of NASA's strategic planning for decades, but it came into its own during the Reagan administration. In 1984, the president gave a speech outlining a new space initiative with an internationally created space station at its core. The outpost would be named *Freedom*. But as the years dragged on and administrations changed, once again NASA found itself at the mercy of an underfunded initiative. Ever since John Kennedy's "Moon Speech" in 1961, presidents have sought to recapture similar glories by making their own daring space proclamations. None has come close, and none has resulted in a similar gush of funding and support. In short, they have been long on talk and short on commitment.

And so it was with the space station. The agency worked on plans and began the construction of specific components, all destined to be lofted into orbit by the space shuttle. But as the years went by and the project languished, it became clear that the desired orbital workshop would not succeed as envisioned. Inviting the Russians to participate gave the effort some political cover, reaching out to an old enemy.

So including the Russians became a no-brainer. With the collapse of the Soviet Union in 1991, selling the idea to skeptics in Congress became far easier. The Soviets had lofted many more stations than we had (albeit smaller ones) and had experience in modular design with Mir. They also had large rockets that could lift heavy loads more cheaply than the shuttle could. And, perhaps most compellingly, they had hardware of their own, originally built for a Mir II space station but not used, sitting in storage. It was a perfect match.

What the Russians did not have ample supplies of was cash. Other partners were recruited who had at one time entertained space platform ideas of their own, all of which had been stillborn or delayed. The Europeans, through their own European Space Agency, had been designing an outpost of their own called *Columbus*. The small station, planned to be about 15 by 25 feet, was originally to have been serviced by the European Hermes mini-shuttle. But like the Japanese and others, all of whom had looked on while the United States built and flew its own shuttle, they decided to shelve the space plane project. Space shuttles were more trouble than they were worth. So the *Columbus* was incorporated into the ISS, and *Hermes* remained stillborn in French file cabinets.

SOLUTION:

Forge an unprecedented alliance between the United States and European and Asian powers, especially Russia, to finance and build a truly international space station.

As Europe went, so did Japan. Its Japanese Experiment Module, nicknamed *Kibo* (Hope), was also to operate with a space plane, this one of Japanese design. But in the end, they too decided to join the ISS venture and shipped their hardware skyward in three shuttle flights. It would end up being the largest single ISS module.

The Russian *Mir 2* designed modules were the oldest, having been started (at least on paper) in 1976. This design had gone through various iterations that included a huge satellite-killing laser for deployment against U.S. spacecraft. But with the end of the USSR, planning returned to a more peaceful mission, and it was merged with the ISS program.

NASA's station designs were not proceeding unfettered, either. From 1984 to 1987, as the design was being circulated, commented upon, and finalized, the Department of Defense once again remembered that it too had always wanted a space station and demanded full and open access to the orbital platform. NASA was not pleased, and the arguments raged in Washington. It got so bad that a group of NASA employees put together an allegedly serious proposal to pull the backup *Skylab* out of the Smithsonian and simply fly that. The plan was, of course, shelved.

OLD ENEMIES, NEW PARTNERSHIPS

By 1998, the decisions had been made and real work in space could begin. The Russians launched their modules on their own rockets. Their first module, *Zarya*, supplied power, propulsion, and guidance to the station as it was being assembled. Once the station became operational, *Zarya* would be primarily a storage space.

Two weeks later, the U.S. Unity module was launched in a shuttle and docked with *Zarya*. Then in 2000, another Russian module, *Zvezda*, was launched. This marked the real beginnings of a true space station: the module provided sleeping accommodations, a toilet, a galley, life support, and communications capability. Now crews could begin to arrive and stay.

Later that year, a Russian Soyuz delivered the first three crew members to the station in a mission called *Expedition 1*. Two shuttle flights, delivering large structural truss units, bracketed the crew's arrival. For the first time, multiple crews in multiple spacecraft were working with robotic arms and spaceborne astronauts to build an orbiting space platform.

Over the next two years, construction was continuous. Then, in 2003, the shuttle *Columbia* broke up during reentry, and the shuttle program stalled. But in 2005 the long-awaited *Columbus* module and the final segment of the Japanese *Kibo* were carried aloft by the shuttle and mated to the station. It had at last become a fully functioning, large-scale platform.

By the time the construction and addition phase of the station was completed in 2011, the station effort had consumed more than 1,000 hours of extravehicular activities, 159 components had been installed, and the station had become the most expensive man-made object in history.

CHALLENGE:

How to construct a huge structure in orbit with pieces from a half-dozen nations.

All along, even when the shuttles were flying, resupply was being done by a variety of craft. The Russians used an ingenious unmanned spacecraft called *Progress* that docked robotically and delivered tons of cargo. The Europeans and Japanese also have unmanned cargo carriers that make trips to the station. Finally, in 2012, shortly after the end of space shuttle operations, the private U.S. company SpaceX docked its *Dragon* space capsule with the ISS and began a schedule of supply deliveries. The *Dragon* provides an added bonus of being able to return items to Earth for analysis and disposal. SpaceX is the first private venture of its kind in history, and it promises to become a primary supplier of both crew delivery and resupply to the station as it moves forward.

SOLUTION:

Design the station to be modular—individual components will be attached to a giant trusswork in space. Each nation would select its own launch vehicle that best fills its needs (most chose the shuttle). Assemble the delivered components in orbit.

The ISS is now operating in its ultimate form. It is capable of safely supporting a crew of six on a long-term basis. It would weigh almost a million pounds if it were on the Earth's surface—it's 239 feet long and 356 feet wide, and it has almost 30,000 cubic feet of pressurized volume where astronauts can live, work, and sleep. It's been continually occupied for about 13 years, and it is scheduled to operate until at least 2020, and probably 2024, at which point it will be either repurposed or disassembled and deorbited. The Russians are developing a plan to utilize parts of the station to spin off a newer design that is more suited to their purposes.

AN UNPRECEDENTED ALLIANCE

The international partnership has become the most successful of its kind in history. No fewer than 15 nations participate, and of these, some countries support multiple components. The list of international partners includes the original designers and builders: the United States, Russia, Canada, and Japan. Research and flight partners include Belgium, Denmark, France, Germany, Italy, Netherlands, Norway, Spain, Sweden, Switzerland, and the United Kingdom. As regards international space agencies, the European Space Agency (composed of a number of the above), Japan's JAXA (their version of NASA), and Russia's Roscosmos are fully engaged. India began cooperation efforts in 2011. It's an impressive array of participants, and it has already been managed and maintained for more than 20 years. The only major player missing is China, which is currently under consideration.

The station has quietly provided a stable platform for an enormous amount of scientific research in many fields. Some of the most profound work has been in biology, immunology, and other health-related pursuits. Examples include a new and revolutionary treatment for muscular dystrophy, one of the most tenacious diseases to affect children; new vaccines for maladies as varied as salmonella and staph infections, the latter being one of the most persistent killers in modern hospitals; and vastly improved manufacture of various drugs that are able to be better targeted than past versions. None of these developments would be possible on Earth's surface. Moving beyond this are many projects in metallurgy, fluid dynamics, and biosciences, and much basic research on things both Earthly and cosmic.

The ISS has not been kept secret, but it has also never received the acclaim and worldwide attention that it deserves. Perhaps this is due to its very long life span and the fact that we have gotten used to it wheeling overhead every 90 minutes. But do yourself a favor some weekend: look up the sighting schedule (available online under "ISS sightings"), find somewhere as dark as you can, and look up into the night sky. Soon, at the appointed time, you will see one of humanity's greatest achievements as it slowly moves from one horizon to the other, taking an apparently leisurely trip across the night sky, but in reality traveling in excess of 17,000 mph. And then think of the people up there and the incredible work they are doing.

Then, imagine what we could do if we put our minds to it. With passion, boldness, and the resulting innovation, the possibilities are endless.

INNOVATIONS

- Managed to make the Space Station *Freedom* an international effort. This involved modification of existing hardware and integration of foreign-built systems, each with its unique requirements.
- Provided modular design elements, all of which could be hauled into orbit by the U.S. space shuttle and Russian rockets.
- Designed all components and modules to be assembled via traditional docking, by use of the robotic arm on the shuttle, or by astronauts during EVA. This last requirement was tricky, but it worked perfectly.
- Successfully managed an assembly of 15 international partners on a continuing basis.
- Integrated U.S. commercial and various international resupply flights with an array of spacecraft types.
- Conceived and exploited numerous practical research projects for the station, which have already led to advances in medical treatment and prevention of disease.
- With Russia, planning follow-on mission utilizing some existing space station structures.

CHAPTER 17

NEWSPACE: CAPITALISM SHINING BRIGHT

CHALLENGES

- Find a role for private industry within a leaner, more cautious government environment.
- Define an overall mission objective for the agency, leaving routine orbital operations to the private sector.
- Find ways to meet NASA's exploration goals with diminished budgets.
- Learn to coexist with the new private space operators in a robust entrepreneurial environment.
- Face challenges from, and encourage partnerships with, foreign space agencies.

NOT YOUR FATHER'S NASA

As NASA moves into the twenty-first century, the agency faces new and unprecedented challenges. The shuttles have been decommissioned because of the expense of launching, refurbishment, and maintenance—it was an effective program, but one that was expensive and never lived up to its promise. The follow-on project from 2004, the Constellation lunar program, has been canceled because of projected cost overruns and the perception of an uncertain outcome. Oddly, what has replaced it is a not dissimilar program, NASA's Space Launch System, a Saturn V–class heavy booster. The Orion capsule slated to sit atop it is the only part of the Constellation moon rocket that survived that program's demise. Meanwhile the shuttles have joined the remaining Saturn Vs in museums across the country. Future generations may wonder what all the fuss was about.

A part of this uncertain future is the difficulty of defining a new target or objective. Do we want to return to the moon? Do we want to visit near-Earth asteroids? Do we want to continue relatively safe operations in low Earth orbit, where the International Space Station resides? Or . . . do we want to go to Mars and beyond?

CHALLENGE:

How to fill the gap left by decommissioned space shuttles and an underfunded NASA.

NASA has no shortage of clever people, and they do not lack motivation. The same breed of brilliant and bold-thinking visionaries exists today as did in the past. But their ideas are muted by concerns about budgets and shifting priorities, and their proposals are often shelved because of a perceived lack of public and congressional support. Nervous senior executives must tread with care to avoid the displeasure of politicians, powerful business entities, and at times their own leadership. The agency accountants also know that 1/2 of 1 percent of the national budget (Apollo at its peak consumed almost 5 percent) is just not enough to undertake great endeavors. In short, a brilliant, forward-thinking organization filled with brilliant, inspired people is hamstrung by political whims and promised budgets that never materialize.

But out of this has come something new and wonderful. Into the breach have jumped a number of private entrepreneurs, most prominently Elon Musk of SpaceX. At a time when people who should have known better said, "A private company founded by an Internet billionaire is going to build a rocket? And a space capsule? That can carry astronauts? Impossible!" Musk has pushed ahead against great odds to make his dream a reality. His rockets are evolving to become as reliable as any being flown, his space capsules rugged and safe, and his ability to maneuver them to the space station (to which they carry cargo) sublime. His safety record with NASA is nearly perfect, and his success rate is enviable. And he is not stopping there, for like any good visionary, once he reaches one milestone, another pops into view. His ultimate goal? Nothing less than the settlement of Mars.

SOLUTION:

Spend NASA dollars to encourage private industry to co-invest and build a commercial infrastructure to support NASA projects in space.

THE NEW '49ERS

And Musk is not alone. Other companies, founded by the same visionaries and enthusiasts who were often branded dreamers and nut jobs in the 1980s, are flourishing. Planetary Resources was founded by Peter Diamandis and Eric Anderson, both seasoned space entrepreneurs. They were joined by film director James Cameron and Larry Page, Google's cofounder. The company's charter is to find and mine asteroids, among other things. It has been quietly working to change the face of unmanned space exploration, and recently ran the largest Kickstarter crowdfunding campaign yet to fund the first private orbiting telescope.

Joining them is Deep Space Industries (DSI). A smaller company, DSI was founded by Rick Tumlinson and David Gump, also both seasoned space entrepreneurs. Their previous efforts include the first advertising campaign in space on the Russian Mir space station. They share the goal of mining asteroids and have expanded their area of interest to include refueling satellites with the elements they find in space.

Both companies can theoretically benefit from the broad availability of water ice, metals, and other useful elements found on asteroids. From water come rocket fuel and air to breathe. Metals can be smelted into spacecraft parts. And since both water and metal are exceptionally heavy and expensive to launch into space, the future of asteroid mining and utilization would seem to be assured for those who venture forth successfully. Both companies have also shown interest in participating in planetary defense against asteroids and other dangerous space objects.

CHALLENGE:

Find ways to make money in space.

And there are private operators getting into the space tourism business. Richard Branson's Virgin Galactic aims for suborbital hops to be flown sometime in 2014 or 2015. Xcor's Lynx space plane, looking somewhat like a miniature space shuttle, is scheduled to take single passengers into space shortly thereafter. Sierra Nevada Corporation has built and is testing the Dreamchaser, a small shuttle-style space plane patterned after NASA's design studies of the 1960s. Boeing, a more traditional supplier of NASA hardware, has built its own capsule for commercial space travel. And Jeff Bezos, of Amazon.com fame, has a company named Blue Origin that is building a variety of crewed spacecraft components for eventual orbital flights, similar to the market that SpaceX is assaulting.

SOLUTION:

A combination of government contracts for NASA project support and new markets such as space tourism and asteroid mining. Find existing needs and exploit them; where there are none, invent them.

What is NASA's response to these commercial challengers? The space agency has, after much debate, wisely begun to spend money both on development assistance and to buy future flight contracts. NASA has always procured its spacecraft from private aerospace firms like Rockwell, Martin, and Grumman, but through fully funded contracts. In the new model, companies invest substantial risk capital of their own before receiving help from NASA.

AND WHAT OF NASA?

At the same time, NASA continues to struggle with development of its own launch and spacecraft systems. Working with a general notion that low Earth orbit can be serviced by private and foreign suppliers (as it now is by the Russians), NASA is in the process of building the Space Launch System (SLS), a giant booster that will give the old Saturn V a serious run for its money. In fact, the ultimate form of the SLS should be able to lift substantially more than the Saturn, if all goes according to plan. The Orion capsule, left over from the cancelled Constellation project, will ride atop the rocket. It will be capable of flights to the moon and beyond. It will also be, by far, the most expensive launch system ever developed. Development continues even as the merits of the system are continuously debated.

CHALLENGE:

How to fund new projects in the twenty-first century while maintaining those from the twentieth.

So in the calculus of twenty-first-century U.S. spaceflight, there is a working balance emerging between the private sector and government-developed spaceflight. NASA will let contracts to the commercial operators until (and if) they find enough ways to generate revenue that they can operate free of government assistance. This will leave NASA free to explore beyond Earth orbit, and to reenter deep space for the first time since the 1970s. At least, that's the plan.

SOLUTION:

Turn over flights and deliveries to Earth orbit to the commercial companies, leaving NASA free to concentrate on larger ventures deeper in space.

NASA is a government agency and, as such, has always been at the whims and mercies of the executive and legislative branches, and by extension a fickle citizenry. Its support has been inconsistent, with budgets often arriving too late and too small. This year's project will be paid for by next year's budget, when or if it arrives. It is a shabby way to do business in such a high-tech arena, and it is the same thinking that compromised the space shuttle and led to its dangerous operational history. But for now, this system of appropriations and funding is what we have.

Few countries do better. Japan has largely given up on its ambitions for human spaceflight. India is at least a decade away. Europe has fielded various plans for manned vehicles over the years—the

HOTOL, a whale-shaped space plane; *Hermes*, a smaller mini-shuttle; and a few private ventures that have not yet made it off paper and into metal—but for now has settled for robotic exploration. Russia continues to operate the 50-year-old Soyuz space capsule and has modest plans for robotic exploration, but it is for now largely relegated to a for-hire role in space access.

The one exception to the pattern is China. This rapidly growing program has repeatedly flown its own astronauts, sometimes called "Taikonauts," in a modified Russian Soyuz capsule. With this, it has established an orbital presence and is building a small space station of its own, with plans to go to the moon.

EVOLUTION, NOT REVOLUTION

CHALLENGE:

For private industry to avoid R&D dead ends and rapidly and cheaply bring about increased access to space.

Budgets and priorities aside, one reason we are not seeing innovation in spaceflight along the lines of the Apollo era is the same reason that commercial airliners look generally similar to they way they did in 1970. The simple fact is that for the sort of ventures we are likely to undertake in the next decade or two, the designs that have already been pioneered and tried—capsules and winged space planes—work well. The hard work of early R&D has been done by government, and the results are available to the new players in the field. The coming decade will be a period of refinement and evolution. NASA and the USSR did the heavy lifting in the 1960s; others are benefiting greatly from this pioneering knowledge, and will continue to build upon it.

This is not to say that there are not new and revolutionary designs to come. Nuclear propulsion, private space yachts, and even permanently cycling interplanetary liners are on the drawing boards. But for the near future, designs based on successful past operations fill out the spaceflight portfolio.

> **SOLUTION:**
>
> Draw on hard-earned knowledge and experience by NASA and Russia to design improved spacecraft based on successful designs and programs.

At the moment, NASA's brightest star is arguably the unmanned planetary exploration program. Bolstered by the brilliant success of *Curiosity* and the sky crane system that delivered it, the Mars rover has paved the way for others to follow using similar technologies. And the outer planets are still on the menu as well—missions are underway or being planned to move farther into deep space, scouting Pluto, further investigating comets and asteroids, and perhaps even landing on the icy moons of Jupiter to extend the search for life.

For the time being, however, JPL is proceeding along three carefully designed pathways. First, continue creating new programs as budgets allow, with priority being given to (1) Earth observation missions that create a direct and immediate benefit, (2) Mars exploration missions, since the planet is relatively close by and the most Earthlike of the other planets, and (3) the rest of the solar system. Second, work to partner with private industry and other outside entities to maximize efficiency and cost reduction while spurring innovation. Third, continue to work the "legacy missions," such as Voyager, which continues to send home data from the edge of the solar system. There is only so much money to go around, so like the rest of NASA they must carefully triage their operations.

THE ROAD AHEAD

So what is NASA's next *great* adventure? Where will we send human crews next? What will be the realm in which the agency extends its creative forces, innovating its way to new places beyond Earth orbit? That is under heavy debate. Some people want to return to the moon and stay there, mining it for its resources (which may include usable amounts of water, metals, and helium 3, a possible fuel for nuclear fusion). Others think it's time to take the great leap and head off to Mars. They do not fear the problems of radiation, isolation, zero-gravity living conditions, and all the other dragons at the edge of the map. They feel that we must recapture the spirit of the space race and go for broke.

And still others would have us shut down our space station, bring the astronauts home, dismantle NASA's crewed space efforts, and be done with it.

But innovation and innovators do not stand still for the doubters. What NASA does not undertake, the private sector may ultimately pursue for profit. Some of those dollars will come from tourism, some from biotech, and some from asteroid mining. Plans are being made by private firms to grow stem cells on the space station, and possibly new strains of plant and animal cells that are resistant to drought and disease. In addition, 3-D printing is rewriting the spaceflight manual, ultimately allowing components and even food to be made in space from elements found in space. Google's Lunar XPRIZE challenge, a competition amongst private, nongovernment players to land on and traverse the moon with a small robot by 2015, has spawned more than 30 competitors from places as diverse as Chile, Malaysia, and Russia. This is just a small sampling of the forward thinking coming from the twenty-first century's most fertile minds.

And where do these forward-looking entrepreneurial innovators come from? Some of them are within NASA; others are from the outside. Many were formerly among NASA's ranks. Still others are recent graduates from college programs in Silicon Valley, the northeast, the Midwest, Europe, Asia, and just about anywhere you can imagine. Most have benefitted greatly from the innovations pioneered by NASA over the five decades of its existence. From aerospace to universities to secondary school programs, the space agency has long been a principal supporter of science, engineering, and mathematics in the United States and beyond. Within its limits, NASA continues this mission today. With luck (and proper appropriations), this support will continue into the future.

There is room for countless newcomers. Long after *Star Trek*'s "final frontier" catchphrase entered the popular lexicon, we have at last reached a point where that frontier, in so many ways reminiscent of the American West of the eighteenth century, is finally cracking open and becoming available to ambitious entrepreneurs, and soon, via private spaceflight operators, regular folks. And, as with the opening of the West, there is a profound role for government support.

Whatever form NASA's future may take, it will always include large measures of boldness, daring, and passion. This is because space exploration cannot prosper without innovation powered by these traits. And exploration, after all, is NASA's primary mission.

INNOVATIONS

- Reduced overall expenditures, reduced staff, and cut programs to accommodate tighter budgets while still designing and operating cutting-edge programs.
- Canceled a new lunar rocket and lunar lander, but continued development of the Orion space capsule for other uses; initiated a new super-booster to provide deep-space access.
- Redefined the mission to focus on asteroids and an eventual crewed Mars mission.

- Promoted development of commercial companies to provide access to low Earth orbit.
- Supported programs of outsourcing space station crew flights and rocket parts to Russia.
- Trimmed but maintained robotic planetary exploration, with emphases on Mars (closest target) and Earth orbit (most direct benefit).

CHAPTER 18

COMING HOME: BRINGING NASA's LESSONS TO YOUR BUSINESS

IN THE WORKPLACE

We have seen many examples of how innovation has worked inside NASA to drive the exploration of space. We have further looked at the new surge of private companies building on NASA's experience and forging their own pathways to space and NASA's support of and experience with them. It's been a wide swath of history, from 1957 through today. But how do we take these lessons and apply them here, on Earth, in our own businesses and workplaces?

NASA remains a government-funded agency. It has historically been centrally controlled and managed, although each field center has a degree of autonomy. Overall, the NASA of today bears only a fading resemblance to the space agency that flew to the moon—it has grown up (some would assert that it's simply grown old). The mainstays are there; the boldness, daring, and passion that infused NASA in those years remains in a more mature and altered form. But so much else has changed.

For one thing, it is no longer an agency of white men in starched shirts and skinny ties. A visit to today's Mission Control, for example, will reveal a mélange of men and women of all ages and ethnicities. This is true across the agency. Likewise, the backgrounds from which these people come—whether it be traditional middle-class suburban America, a forested township in Tennessee, a neighborhood in Mumbai, or some other part of the world—are equally diverse. This is not your father's NASA.

However, the agency has also changed in some ways that are less desirable. While more demographically liberal, it is a more operationally conservative operation than it was in the past. This is in part a natural and proper outgrowth of experience and the maturing of space exploration. NASA doesn't *need* to take the same chances it did in the 1960s. It doesn't *need* to prepare and fly missions every 10 weeks, as it did in the Gemini years, to test orbital endurance and rendezvous techniques. And it does not *need* to be as daring as in the past.

Nor would budgets allow it to embrace these things, even if they were beneficial. At the height of the Apollo program, the space program devoured about 5 percent of the national budget. For many years now, it's been more like 0.5 percent. That's a huge difference. And don't think that just because we know more about what we are doing, it has gotten cheaper—many space activities cost far more because of increased safety specifications, more elaborate equipment, and greatly increased labor costs. Overall, it is a testament to the dedication of the workforce that the agency is able to accomplish what it does.

There is one more key element: NASA management. When you speak to the workforce about the management of the space agency, you will hear opinions across the range from deep admiration to frustration with an aging bureaucracy. But there's one thing most people will agree on: NASA strives to encourage innovation. The techniques vary among field centers and departments. One common theme is freedom—most departments that are engaged in planning future activities are given something akin to a "blue-sky" mandate. Think big, and don't just think outside the box, start beyond the box. Think beyond three dimensions, if you will.

Robert Manning of the JPL's Mars program cautions that there is a tension between extremes here, however. Innovation is highly prized during the proposal and conceptualization stages of a project, but once the program is approved and budgeted, things become more complex. "We are spending public funds," he says, "so innovation for its own sake is not an option. It must serve the project at hand, and risk is tightly managed. It's a bit of yin and yang; and with an idea like sky crane, the concerns were profound up front."

LESSONS FROM YESTERYEAR

During the space race, NASA's golden age to many observers, innovation was encouraged in a number of ways. First came need-based innovation: the task set before the agency in 1961 was so vast, so demanding, that the new and original became commonplace. Outside-the-box thinking was the norm, then these ideas had to be wrestled into some kind of box to make them reality. Budgets were coming hot and heavy, and the money was there to correct errors made along the way.

The second was innovation at the end of a sharp stick. An example would be when George Low, then managing the Apollo Spacecraft Program Office, insisted that von Braun approve the "all-up" testing of the Saturn V—there simply was neither the time nor the resources to do the more traditional incremental testing. The weight-saving program surrounding Grumman's Lunar Module also comes to mind.

Finally, there was innovation of the more blue-sky variety. Programs like the Apollo Applications Office, which thought up missions like a flyby of Venus with Apollo hardware and various other schemes, intended to use the designs of the space race for other missions. These were innovative missions that were flown only on paper for years, with one notable exception being *Skylab*.

It should be noted that at least in part, managing (and nurturing) innovation is difficult to separate from NASA's traditional approach to management. James Webb, NASA administrator from 1961 to 1968, felt that management was a science and could be applied like one. His team recruited personnel from the Air Force and Navy to introduce ideas and utilize experiences in what became known as "systems engineering," communicating between, and sometimes managing personnel of, different groups, working cultures, and organizations. This approach was further refined by incorporating experience from managers at JPL, which had spent its first two decades as both a private (Caltech) and a military (U.S. Army) organization. The unique management culture "percolated up" into the broader NASA hierarchy. This topic is beyond the scope of this book, but it did (and does) have a bearing on how innovation is handled within NASA.

Travel across the United States and visit the NASA field centers distributed across the country. At any of them—the Johnson Space Center, the Kennedy Space Center, the Ames Research Center in northern California, or any of the others—you will find people conceptualizing grand new programs with exciting and unique goals. It is an inspiring experience just to spend time in the same room with these folks—they define outside-the-box thinking. Their minds live anywhere from Earth orbit to the surface of Mars to the moons of Saturn and beyond. How many of these wonderful visions will make their way into reality is always the profound question.

AND FROM TODAY

Despite the challenges of low budgets and risk aversion, thoughtful innovation does ascend through the system. There is always time later to rein in ideas to fit budget and schedule parameters. But if you don't go large at the beginning, you will never achieve greatness. This was phrased with eloquence by Dr. Jakob van Zyl, associate director of project formulation and strategy at JPL:

> *I want to first be completely unconstrained and think about what are the kinds of things [we can do] that will touch humanity. Then we can figure out how to make it affordable. We are spending taxpayer money after all.*

This is a quietly voiced grand vision, and it points us toward some lessons from NASA's decades of leadership in space.

FIRST, BE BOLD

Words like *bold, daring,* and *passionate* are not always associated with NASA today . . . but they should be. Given proper resources, NASA has shown boldness in its five decades of work in space that make most industries pale by comparison. By its very nature, space exploration is a dangerous business, and boldness is required to take even the first steps: considering where, then how, to go.

When President Kennedy sent a three-year-old NASA the mandate to go to the moon within nine years, it was an audacious goal. As was said at the time, the engineers didn't even know what they didn't know. The metallic alloys, the machining equipment, the methodologies, and much more were not even on the drawing boards. And yet, by mid-1969, the manned landings had been achieved. Astronauts would walk on that airless world six times.

The shuttle, compromised though it was, represented a complete and total departure from what had gone before: a winged, reusable space plane that was capable of hauling heavy cargo into space and, when necessary, back to Earth. It bore little resemblance to the Saturn V moon rocket and shared few components with the Apollo program. Yet it fulfilled its mission for the next 30 years, albeit at a premium price.

Then the International Space Station came into being, the most expensive object ever created. This football-field-sized machine wheels overhead every 90 minutes, providing up to six occupants with a place to live, work, and conduct research for the betterment of humanity. It is a triumph of engineering, international cooperation, and accomplishment.

The boldness of these programs, and of the people who created them, can be an inspiration to all of us in daily life, not just our business endeavors. When Wernher von Braun and his predecessors first spoke of rocketing to other worlds, they were met with skepticism at best and derision at worst. But within a few decades, the goal had been accomplished, and more than once. This was bold and creative thinking.

When we set out to bring innovation to our own workplaces and businesses, it is often with some degree of risk—sometimes minor, sometimes great. But if we believe in our ideas, if we have confidence in ourselves, and if we are bold in our plans and assertions, great things can happen. Without boldness, they will not.

NEXT, BE DARING

Bold plans require daring execution. Some definitions of *daring* are "adventurous or audaciously bold," "boldly unconventional," and "defiant and challenging." Do these sound like assets and virtues in the task of innovation? They should.

When NASA accepted the mission of traveling to the moon, it took tremendous amounts of daring on the part of dozens of top executives, managers, and other leaders to make the dream a reality. The bold goal was followed by daring execution. Likewise, so did a more recent example: landing 2013's *Curiosity* rover on Mars. The bold decision to land a drivable machine on its wheels with a rocket pack, with a couple of thousand potential points of failure, took a lot of convincing to pull off—not just with NASA upper management, but with the American scientific community and the public at large. The idea just looked crazy when it was presented, but the daring of the people who invented it, and their raw determination to make it happen, are inspiring.

Without daring execution, bold ideas languish and are useless.

AND PROCEED WITH PASSION

Visit any NASA facility. Talk to the engineers; observe the flight controllers; chat with the thousands of people who design the missions, build the hardware, pay the bills, download and process the data, and all the rest. To a person, if you look closely, you will find a driving passion behind what he or she does. It may be harder to spot in some than in others, for passion can be a difficult thing to maintain in any government entity, even one as exceptional as NASA. The money is scarce, and the odds are often stacked against them. Any one of these people could make more money in private industry, yet they choose to stay with NASA. Why? It might be the exciting nature of the work; it might be that they are fulfilling a childhood dream. It might even, for some in the twilight of their careers, be the promise of a pension that they have earned with 30 years of service. But scratch the surface, and you will find passion within.

The Grumman engineers who designed the Lunar Module, that most difficult of spacecraft to conceive and build, did so with great passion. The company had staked its reputation, and even its future, on the successful design and construction of a spacecraft that nobody even knew how to build when they started. It took rich reserves of passion and persistence to follow the Herculean task to its conclusion. But they did, and none of Grumman's machines failed in flight; indeed, without the Lunar Module on *Apollo 13*, the astronauts would have died within hours of the explosion that robbed them of the use of their Apollo capsule.

Likewise, the people who designed and fabricated the heat-shielding tiles for the space shuttle had great passion. Nobody was quite sure if the design would work. The idea seemed outlandish at the beginning—cover the bulk of a huge space plane with fragile little ceramic tiles, and affix them with *glue*? But the math checked out, the tests confirmed their beliefs, and the passion within them allowed the program to enjoy a high rate of success.

Greatness in innovation is never easy.

There are countless other examples, some that were mentioned in this book and many more that were not. But spaceflight is by definition a difficult thing to accomplish, as we have seen again and again in the remarkable successes and, perhaps more poignantly, in the rare failures in the American space program. But no other entity has even come close to succeeding as NASA has in these undertakings, and this is a testament to a number of things. Paramount among them is the passion of those involved in their execution, a passion that is supported and fueled by the system of free enterprise that spawned the undertaking in the first place. This could not have occurred within any other system at any other time in human experience—witness the results of the space race between America and the Soviet Union. Both systems gave it their all; the results speak for themselves.

LIVING THE INSPIRATION

When you are faced with a challenge, large or small, in the workplace or your own private activities, think on the accomplishments described in this book and the nature of the people and the system that allowed them to occur. Reflect on the boldness of the vision, the daring of the execution, and the passion that drove it. Use this great gift to your own advantage, and achieve great things. Innovation is where you find it; it is a serendipitous process that cannot be quantified. But when the spark is ignited within you, bring the qualities that took America to the moon, built a magnificent space station, and explored the planets to your greatest dreams. And then, watch how innovation can take root in your own endeavors.

INDEX